THE SECRET WAR DIARY OF A WORTHING SOLDIER

To David

Thanks for your interest in our book.

Gerry
Bob

Gerald Tiller and Bob Wragg

This amazing story can now be told

Published by Albion Press
54 Hollingdean Road,
Brighton, BN2 4AA

ISBN 978-0-9558103-7-4

© Copyright: Bob Wragg, August 2012

All rights reserved.
No part of this book may be reproduced, stored in any retrieval system or transmitted, in any form or by means, electronic, mechanical photocopying or otherwise without the permission of the publishers.

Printed in Great Britain by
One Digital, Brighton

ABOUT THE AUTHORS

GERALD TILLER

Gerry is the author of the original Diary. He grew up in Worthing and prior to joining the Army he took up an apprenticeship as a carpenter. He served in the Army from 1943 until 1948 and on leaving returned to Worthing with his wife who he met in Germany during the war. They shared a happy marriage of over fifty years until her death in 2005. Gerry spent his working life as a carpenter and engineer and his garden workshop is a testament to his great skills. It contains many examples of his work that he has produced over the years including a working scale model of a steam engine, tender and coaches which he designed and built.

Gerry is 86 years old and despite his poor health he enjoys gardening and looking after his two cats. Although he greatly misses his beloved wife Margarete he is very thankful for the full and happy life he has had. He is indebted to Bob for his help in writing his story.

BOB WRAGG

Bob Wragg was born in Hertfordshire in 1941 and lived in Harpenden until his early teens when his family moved to Southampton. He attended King Edward VI School and on leaving spent two years as a crew member on a research ship in Antarctica. He then joined the Metropolitan Police serving for two years in uniform and then ten years in the C.I.D in east and south London and at New Scotland Yard. He was Security Manager for three national retail companies and a hotel chain before joining Cunard as Security Officer on QE2. On leaving the sea Bob was appointed Branch Manager of a national driving school and also qualified as a driving instructor specialising in teaching disabled people to drive.

Bob's first book 'Jacob's Ladder', telling the story of his terminally ill grandson, was published in 2009 and this is his second book. He is a member of the West Sussex Writers' Club. It has been a pleasure and honour for him to have helped Gerry to produce this book.

Bob has been married to Anne for 46 years and they have four children and five grandchildren. He lives in Worthing, West Sussex and his hobbies include writing, reading and watching most sports.

PREFACE

This is the story Of Gerald Tiller, a young soldier who kept a secret Diary throughout the Second World War and it is remarkable in many ways.

Gerry knew that keeping such a Diary was very risky, not only could he have been in trouble with the Army if it was discovered, but if captured by the Germans he might well have been interrogated or even worse. He kept the Diary hidden at the bottom of a toolbox and wrote it with a gold-nibbed fountain pen which he still has today; the biro had yet to be invented. Getting ink for his pen was a constant challenge and as Gerry says, "I used to nick it from shops, schools, anywhere I could find it!"

Obviously it was difficult to write at times, particularly when under fire, but most of the time Gerry managed to record the events as he experienced them. He made short notes in a small Diary and then, when he had time, wrote more detailed accounts in larger exercise books. When writing the book Gerry and I both thought it important that his actual Diary should be re-produced exactly as he wrote it, including any spelling or grammatical errors.

The Diary contains very few of Gerry's thoughts at the time about what he experienced and witnessed and there were several incidents which he quite wisely did not record for security reasons. However, despite the passing years, many of the events are still vivid in Gerry's memory and in writing this book he wanted to reflect on what his thoughts about them were, not only then, but today. He now tells of several events about which he was sworn to secrecy at the time and which affected him greatly for many years; they even produce tears when he talks about them today.

This is not just the story of Gerry and his comrades fighting through France, Belgium, Holland and Germany, it is also a remarkable love story. He tells of how he met his German wife, Margarete, and despite all the odds, managed to keep their relationship secret, married and subsequently settled in England. Above all, this is an account of a young English lad going to war, it is not a story of war strategy or battle leaders, it is a very honest account of Gerry's war. He tells of sad and happy times and of events that most soldiers experienced, some of which may shock the reader.

In researching and writing this book I have spent many happy hours talking to Gerry about his Diary and life and recording his thoughts. Like most heroes – yes, all those who went through the two World Wars were heroes in my eyes - Gerry is reluctant to talk about his experiences. When I read the Diary, graphic though it is, I knew there was much more to tell and I really wanted to know if and how the events had shaped Gerry's life.

The Diary was written many years ago when the events were at the forefront of Gerry's mind, and although he is now 86 years old and his memory is good, he has told his story, with the help of the Diary, to the best of his memory. Where possible, I have researched places and incidents that Gerry talks about.

Someone once said that 'Truth is the first casualty of war.' This is undoubtedly true and there are several incidents which Gerry experienced which certainly seem to give credence to the saying.

I have spent several hours at the National Archives reading the Official War Records of the Royal Engineers 278 Field Company, talked to archivists at the Royal Engineers Museum and visited the Imperial War Museum. Much of what Gerry relates in his story was confirmed by my research. Some of the incidents that he refers to and of which he was told not to talk about at the time but that he secretly recorded in his Diary, such as removing gold bars from a Bank, are not recorded in any Official Records. Research shows that it is hardly surprising that some events that took place throughout the war were not officially recorded – I am sure this applies in any period of war. The one thing that revealed itself to me when reading the Official War Records was the total honesty and integrity with which Gerry wrote his Diary. The Official Records, as one would expect, record dates, times, places, map references and minutiae relating to events involving 278 Company. Gerry's Diary on the other hand tells the story of what happened to him, a typical 'Tommy Atkins' during wartime. One would hardly expect Official Records to report a soldier stealing eggs from a factory in order to supply his mates with a luxury!

It has been a great privilege to have assisted him in writing the book and I thank him for the time he has given me. It is important that men like Sapper Gerald Tiller and his colleagues should never be forgotten; we have our liberty thanks to them and I hope this book is a fitting tribute to them all.

Bob Wragg.

May 2012

FOR MARGARETE
AND
THE LADS OF 278

Many mistakes have I made,
My spelling also not very bright,
The interests that lie within are of places I have stayed,
All these things I thank for my sight.

Many a sorrow owing to loss of life,
But we carry on with a will and a way,
Because we believe in our strife,
That this war will end some day.

Then back to Blighty we will come,
To lead a better life than before,
With our parents and wives an little ones,
Which we hope will carry on for evermore.

SAPPER GERALD TILLER
2 Platoon 278 Royal Engineers
France 1944.

The Famous 15th Scottish Division

Just listen to this story of a bunch of gallant men –

You must have heard about them, time and time again –

The 15th Scottish Division, they fear that glorious name,
And in all their battles they have gained immortal fame.
Each time that we contacted the Boche there is only one decision,
And that, I can assure you, is a win for our division.

We landed here in Normandy prepared to take our chance,
And chase the German Armies completely out of France,
And now, my friends, I think it is quite safe for me to say,
The lads of this division helped to chase them on their way.

The lads they kept hard at it, fighting day and night:
There was nothing that could stop them, not even German might.
The bells of peace will chime again, high in the church's spire,
To let us know of victory and that guns have ceased to fire:

But in the heat of triumph please give a little thought,
To the men that we have lost in the battles that we have fought.

Author unknown

THE OUTBREAK OF WAR

My name is Gerald Tiller and everyone calls me Gerry. I was born on 27th May 1925 in Worthing, Sussex. I had a brother and a sister, both now passed on, and I had a happy childhood. My father was a driver with British Rail and my mother was a housewife. As I grew up I got up to the usual mischief with my mates that lads of that age did but I don't think I was ever any real problem to my parents. When I was fourteen I left school and went to work with a local carpenter and my Dad was pleased that I was learning a trade.

I remember the Second World War starting in 1939 and I suppose people of my age didn't realise or think about what it meant at the time. It was quite exciting to watch the air battles going on in the skies above Worthing and the south coast. I remember watching the huge numbers of German aircraft flying over from France to drop bombs on London and other places and a few hit Worthing.

When I was fifteen I joined the Home Guard which was formed to protect England if the country was invaded and it was made up mainly of men who for various reasons couldn't join the regular Army, usually because of age or medical problems. You had to be sixteen to join but I lied about my age and joined at fifteen. I still worked as a carpenter but was trained in aircraft observation and at night would go on Home Guard duty with other lads up on the hills above Worthing looking down on the surrounding area and out across the English Channel towards France. Our job was to watch out for incoming German enemy aircraft and when identified pass the details on by radio to our HQ. I really enjoyed it; we had some laughs but took our jobs seriously and in some ways I suppose it was a bit like the television programme 'Dad's Army.' A very strange incident happened when I was in the Home Guard.

One night I was on night duty with my mate up on the downs overlooking Worthing and surrounding areas out across the English Channel. We noticed an aerial high up in a tree in the grounds of a big house near the golf course. We reported what we had found to our senior officer and found out later that as a result a man who lived at the house was arrested. We were later told that he was alleged to be a German collaborator.

Evidently he was watching the British aircraft movements and relaying the details to the Germans. He was watched for some time by a security agent from London and eventually caught outside his house in possession of his Morse code transmitter. I don't know what happened to him. At the time my parents had their milk delivered by a chap they quite liked and he also delivered to the 'spy's house'. One day, without warning, he stopped delivering and it turned out that he was the security agent from London who had been employed as a milkman! Dad and I were pleased that a 'spy' had been caught, Mum was sorry because she had lost her 'nice milkman!' I don't think that this incident was ever reported in the local paper which is hardly surprising due to a Government censorship on publishing such information.

I couldn't wait to join the Regular Army and on 1st April 1943, a couple of months before my eighteenth birthday, I signed up. My family and girlfriend were sorry to see me leave Worthing but were so proud of me. I did six weeks basic training at Preston, Lancashire which was quite hard but god fun. I was then sent to the Training Brigade, Royal Engineers at Elgin in Scotland where I remained for about eight or nine months with no leave. The training was very severe but it gave me great confidence which I relied on throughout the war. I learned to lay bridges, defuse land mines and survive in very harsh situations. I became very good at First Aid which later served me well many times when fighting in the front line and looking after casualties. I was issued with a First Aid kit which included scissors, a scalpel, tweezers etc. which I still have today. I also scored very high marks at shooting. On completing my training in Scotland I was posted to 278 Field Engineers 15th Scottish Division in Yorkshire where I stayed until the build up to D-Day.

Before going to Yorkshire I was given a few days leave. I travelled down from Scotland to London and when I was on the train I met two other servicemen. One was a sailor who was going on leave from Scapa Flow and lived in Brighton, the other was in the RAF. We talked a lot about the war and when we arrived at Liverpool Street Station we decided to all get a taxi to Victoria. The first taxi driver we asked would not take us as he said the roads were so bad from the German bombing of London the night before but we managed to get another driver to take us but he charged us quite a lot of money for doing I will never forget that journey because it was the first time I had seen the result of all the bombing that the London people had suffered. There were bombed buildings everywhere, lots were on fire, and the taxi driver had to go quite slowly in order to go over the fire hoses which were all over the roads. Lots of people seemed to be doing what they could to help the firemen and police and others were going to work as usual. It was sad to see how much the Londoners were suffering. Little did I realise at the time that I would later witness a similar picture of the suffering the French, Belgium, Dutch and German civilians experienced from bombing in their countries from our aircraft.

In June 1944 we all knew that something big was about to happen. We were moved down to Paraham Park in Sussex which was very handy for me as it was only a few miles from Worthing and I was able to get home a few times. There was a huge build up of troops and equipment around the area and along the south coast, not just British but American and Canadian. We were then sent to Wanstead Flats on the outskirts of London to await our departure to France. My war was about to begin.

"Tommy V Bosch"
2 Platoon 278 Field boy R.E. BLA

"Normandy"

Started writing 31st July 1944

It was on Friday 16th June that we left Wanstead Flats for Royal Albert docks. We sailed at 6 p.m. for an unknown destination, which is now known to us as France.

The Thames was calm and very busy with other troop ships bound for the open seas. Our ship, which was a "Yanky" one, was called "George Durant". The crew 73 of them were very sociable and jolly. We enjoyed the trip down the Thames to the estuary. We anchored there for forming up as we couldn't go through the Straits unless under cover of darkness, owing to Jerries observation.

The passage through was very rough so we couldn't get a lot of sleep. We rose next morning to find us anchored off Beachy Head. It was a lovely fresh sunny morning of June 18th. The trip during the day was very enjoyable. It was a great sight to see all these vessels going along without being interfered by Jerries fighters, which were very few and far between. We got very sunburnt during the day, as everyone was laying about the deck. As we approached the coast of France there were small vessels busy cruising around giving out orders to the Captains of our convoy. We anchored there at 9 p.m. of Sunday June 18th. Everyone was excited and it took a lot of the Sergeant Major's time in getting everyone below by 10 o'clock, which didn't please him at all. Next morning we rose to find it misty and very choppy, which upset us a little.

This Monday June 19th and jerry decided to worry us. Our ack ack gunners on shore were kept very busy as he sent over these robot planes, which are a menace to us at present. We found out later in the day that they couldn't off load us owing to a storm coming up. We wandered about the ship all day, either *playing cards or admiring the view at times when the mist had cleared. We retired that evening to our bunks, which were very close together. We had a good nights sleep, although the boat rocked violently. We were at the stern of the ship so it was not very pleasant.*

We rose next morning June 20th to find it still rough, so our hopes fell in getting off that day. Myself, I felt very bad and couldn't eat a lot so my place for a day or so was my bunk, as I felt better laying down. Two days pass and still not any signs of being taken off.

On Thursday 22nd June it was a lovely sunny day. Our bombers had been going over for some time now. Jerries ack ack was very great and one of our four engined bombers crashed in flames on the distant hills. Another crash-landed near a village. The Navy was shelling well in land. The sea was a little more settled, so we hope it would improve by the morning.

Next morning Friday 23rd June they started off loading some of the lorries, which pleased us very much. It wasn't until midnight that personal could get off. We were in a half-track vehicle on a tank landing craft, which took us well in to the shore so we didn't get our feet or kit wet. As we expected, the town or village was called Courseulles. We had a little sleep just outside this place, which was our de-waterproofing area.

Nineteen years old and there I was with my mates landing on a beach in France and fighting for my country. What I remember about that moment was I was 'shit scared' and petrified! I will never forget the terrific noise from the German guns which were hidden inside big concrete bunkers on the hills overlooking the beach, also from our aircraft flying over to bomb them. Although I saw many dead and wounded soldiers I didn't have time to think about the possibility of me dying, I just wanted to survive We went up the beach and dived for cover in a trench. Then I remember the Germans were taken out by the constant shelling from off-shore by one of our ships and our lads were cheering. I later heard that thousands of British, American and Canadian troops had landed on the Normandy beaches. Many were killed and injured, but the invasion was successful and it was later described as 'The beginning of the end.'

We rose on the morning of Sat 24th June at 5.30, as we couldn't lose any time in getting to our location. We arrived at our Company harbour after a lot of wasted time in asking different M.P.'s the way. The day passed with us cleaning our kit etc, as it was very dusty on the roads. We were told that evening that we were moving nearer the front to a place called Sackville, which was a small village. It had been knocked about owing to Jerry snipers, which he is very fond of leaving behind. The church had been badly knocked about as a sniper had been worrying our lads, so the gunners opened up on the tower where he was and silenced him.

It was a very hot sunny day of Sunday 25th June, we were kept busy unloading trucks to sort them out as things were loaded on different trucks. Then I was told that I was in the advance party for the big push. We were on a half-track which was to lead the Brigade along a road they thought would be mined. There were four of us; they were Sgt. Greenaway, L/cpl. Banwell and Dvr. Forsythe. We left that evening to go to the Infantry's harbour ready for the morning. We were very worried about the situation, as we were wished good luck, by officers and a padre, so we realized that our job was a sticky one.
Still we had a few hours sleep, which relieved our brains very much.

Throughout the war we slept when we could. Sometimes we went two or three days without any proper sleep. Most of the time I just lay down and quickly dropped off, usually so tired that the guns and noise didn't stop me. I obviously didn't want to die but if it happened while I was asleep I wouldn't know anything about it anyway.

It was 5.30 a.m. on the morning of 26th June. We moved further up the front waiting for our barrage to start. We started to move under our barrage at 7.30 a.m., very keyed up and a little frightened as it was our first time under live fire.

I felt very uncomforted as I was sitting on 120lbs of gun cotton, which is very sensitive stuff. We got on to the road after passing the Canadians on our flank. Our infantry was either side of us in open formation across the cornfields. Jerry was picking off the important ones, such as Officers, N.C.O's and fellows with wireless sets or bagpipes, which is a thing Gerry doesn't like. The Jerry started mortaring our lads who were falling either killed or wounded. Then Sgt. noticed a sniper in the trees and let a full magazine of the bren at him, who fell to the ground much to our delight. We then noticed that the carriers were not behind us so we stopped just in case we were going to fast for them, but they didn't arrive, so as the mortar fire was heavy we turned back to find two carriers and a Churchill tank knocked out by mines on the road, which we had already gone along, so we were very lucky. Then the Sgt. detailed us to clear the remaining mines, which we did with the help of fails on tanks. After that our O.C. sent us forward again nearer Banana Ridge, which was a very hot place for our boys at the time. He then told us that we were to walk the rest of the way into the village of Cheax. We carried with us a mine detector and a bren gun ready for any trouble, which may arise. We arrived in the village to find ruins and water along the roads, which was stopping traffic. There seemed to be nothing at all in the village as far as we were concerned, so we turned back after a good look round.

Then the O.C. ordered our platoon to clear the rubble and water away to let the transport through. So we took 2 half-tracks and a jeep with us with all the stores and mess kit aboard. Well the lads had been working very well when at 6 p.m. Jerry dropped shells right along side one of our half-tracks setting it on fire. The dust and smoke was very bad, so after that it was all one great rush to get out of it as Jerry is very cute in setting ranges on villages he leaves behind him. Our lads got hit very bad. We were notified, by Mr. Baron our officer the following casualties killed:- Cpl. Wilkinson, L/cpl. Jakeman, Sappers. Dobson, Ketnor, Calloway, and Jones, all well liked fellows by the platoon. Those wounded were:- L/cpl. Whitmore, Sappers Cable, Marable and wireless operator Warrick. All these went back to England except Spr. Harris who died of his wounds. We returned back to our harbour area wet and hungry, as the half-track had the rations aboard, so we were in a bad state. The officer asked for lads to go back and bury the dead but they returned as the shellfire was to heavy for them. They were buried by one platoon next day. That evening I was called over by an infantry fellow who had found a Jerry bayonet stuck in the ground with a wire attached, so I went over to look at it but it wasn't a booby trap, so I pulled it out to make sure. Then I was walking across the field when I came upon a Jerry laying full stretch on his back. So I called for an officer which was near at the time to cover me while I woke him up as I had not got any weapon with me. He was wounded in three places by bullets, so the officer sent for the stretcher party but before they dressed *his wounds we searched him just in case and we found 4 rounds of ammo' in his pocket. So it was thought that he was the sniper that had been troubling them all day from the wood near by. He was young and very thin. His clothes were wet through and very thin material. The Red Cross fellows took him away on a jeep to a C.R.S. That night we sat beneath trees in our waterproofs, very cold and wet with very little rest.*

I think that was the first time I saw some of my close friends killed and injured and it turned out to be a very bad day. I started keeping a note in my diary of everyone I knew who had been killed but after a while I stopped as there were so many. Because we were under very heavy shellfire it wasn't always possible to bury our mates and so we would go back later and lay them to rest. I was quite upset but just had to get on with my job and be thankful that I was surviving. I know I did cry at times because of the things I was seeing and I was very scared, but staying in one piece was the important thing. It was that day I came face to face, in a field, with a German soldier for the first time. He was only about my age and injured, he was in a bad way. Although he might well have been one of the enemy snipers who had killed some of my mates earlier at no time did I think of taking revenge or making him pay for their deaths and injuries. I wasn't angry with him and only treated him as I would have wanted to have been treated in the same situation. After all, it wasn't his fault he was in France and killing people any more than it was mine - I was there doing the same thing. I can honestly say that for the whole of the war I didn't see any prisoners treated badly by our soldiers, in fact we helped as many as we could by giving them food and water or treating their injuries. It may have happened but I never saw it. I did hear that the Russians treated prisoners and refugees badly though; some of the German civilians suffered terribly at the hands of the Russians and I saw the result.

We were all aware of the Geneva Convention and how we were to treat prisoners of war and throughout my war I always saw those rules adhered to. I saw thousands of refugees and displaced people fleeing across Europe and I will never forget the helpless looks on some of their faces. I felt so sorry for the children and me and my mates used to give them treats like chocolate if we could.

We woke next morning Tuesday 27th June, very tired and frozen. We stayed there all day digging trenches to get ourselves warm. We heard that snipers were down in the village of Cheax given a good bit of trouble but they were well hidden in the buildings. That night we had a good sleep all though our guns were noisy still they didn't bother us, as we were too tired.

Next morning Wednesday 28th June, we got our kit squared up as much as we could. We had a wash and shave the first for 2 days. That day we were informed that our O.C. Major Asler was killed, with him his batman Spr. Jordan. That evening Jerry made a counter attack with Tiger tanks, which wasn't successful – he lost 4 of them.

Official War Records state that Major Osler (Asler) and five others were killed when a ½ track vehicle was hit. This was a very difficult time, the enemy were constantly counter attacking after their aircraft dropped flares over bridges that we were reconstructing

On Friday night June 30th we moved back out of the line to a new harbour area. Our artillery barrage still very heavy, we had a good nights rest.

On July 2nd Jerry sent over a few shells. We went out in search of water, as most wells were dry near us. A lot of French people coming back with all their belongings on carts and wagons.

On July 3rd it was raining all day. The lads brought some cider back but it was bitter and dry. The only thing was that it quenched your thirst. Our new O.C. arrived, also a few reinforcements. We drew for the pictures, as only a certain number could go. The film was shown in a barn at Cully, it was called "Above Suspicion".

On Wednesday 5th July, we all attended the mobile baths, which we had been looking forward to for a long time, as we were dirty owing to the dust on the roads.

Friday 7th July a big raid by our heavy bombers near Caen. Jerry sent up a lot of flack but we never saw any of our planes do down.

On Sunday 9th July w moved at 9 p.m. with Brigade near Versan, which was under mortar fire at intervals. I took the O.C. along the road 4 miles from Caen. There were a lot of pets running about, also dead cattle laying alongside the road. When we got back to Brigade's harbour Jerry started mortaring it very heavy, so we kept near our trenches. Towards evening one burst near our trucks, puncturing the tyres and killing one driver and injuring 3 others. They were: - Dvr. Parr killed, Cpl. Dipalo, Sprs. Chatterfield and Devine injured. After that they decided to move back to old area as it was getting to hot for us there. Next day we were working on the trucks as they were badly punctured by shrapnel.

I will never forget the sights I saw in and around Caen. Our bombs had flattened the City. Most of the population had left and I can remember the thing that struck me was that everything was silent – just dead cats and dogs lying in the streets and some running about looking for food, there were not even sounds of bird songs. Even today I can remember the smell of death around the place.

On Friday 14th July we moved to a new harbour, nearer the front at a place called St. Mauvieu, a small village. We had a good look round the houses, which were left standing and found some interesting things.

Next day Saturday July 15th, out on a recce for tracks for the big push, near hill 112. It started at 10 p.m. with a great bombardment from our guns. A few Jerry planes were over which kept our gunners busy.

On Sunday 16th it was fine and sunny, so I decided to do my washing, which I was behind with. Went out to find unexploded Jerry bomb, which was bothering some fellows in a field, as they didn't know what it was. Jerries came over that night dropping small bombs, which caused a few fires. Everything proceeding to plan.

On Monday 17th, Jerry came over again with his bombers causing little damage, a few fires started, also a few dogfights during the day.

Tuesday 18th, we moved again to another harbour north of Cheax. Our big heavies were there so we couldn't get much rest. We manned the water point at Corville a small village south of Cheax. We were called upon to blow craters to bury the dead cattle, which was laying about.

Friday 21st, it rained very heavy causing the roads to flood our bury area suffered that day.

On Sat 22nd we went to Bayeux for 6 hours. After wondering about the streets we were surprised to see General Montgomery and Mr Churchill go past in a staff car, lead by a jeep with a siren on to clear the traffic. We went into a café, which was great fun as we couldn't get them to understand us. Anyway we had a small meal costing us 25 francs.

Sunday 23rd July we moved to the other side of Balleroy, a town near St. Lo. There it was fairly quiet, so we had a good nights rest.

Tuesday 25th July our heavy bombers come over in great force, which we like to see as it gives you confidence.

On Thursday we moved to a small bridging sight near Bayeux for a bit of practice bridging. We watched the French women washing their clothes in the river, which was very interesting as I have never seen anything like that before. We moved back to our harbour area for a short while, as I was out next day Sat 29th on a recce for tracks for the tanks.

On Sunday July 30th our bombers raided again owing to a big push going in which went according to plan.

We moved again to a new harbour near Caumont on Sunday evening, which was fairly near the front line. We stayed here for 2 days, then we moved again to a new harbour at a village called Le Loges. Here we met mortar fire from Jerry, so we found our trenches very handy.

On Friday August 4th we moved again to a new harbour near Le Beny Bocage. Here we started again to dig in for a night's sleep, owing to Jerries mortar bombs of which we know too well. The platoon, were out on road maintenance, which we were responsible for. The weather came out to be very hot, so we walked about stripped to the waist in hopes of getting brown.

On Wednesday August 9th we went to see a film called "The Angels Sing", which was very good. It was shown in an old French theatre, which had been badly knocked about.

Next day, Thursday we went for a stroll in search of timer, but we had difficulties as there wasn't much laying about. So we came upon a French farm where some of the lads of another company were making conversation with the people that lived there. One of the fellows could speak French very well, so we were very interested in what was going on. They asked us in to sit at the table. They gave us some cider, which was very nice. The woman was 23 and had got a kiddy of 3 years old. Her husband worked the farm with assistance of a girl of 17, who was very hard worked for her age. They told us some very interesting things. How they lived under the Germans etc. Then she offered us a drink of Cognac, which was very strong but nice. They told us that it had been buried as the Germans take anything they see for themselves. After having a long interesting talk with them we left saying we would return that evening. This we did taking with us our water bottles for milk, in exchange for soap or sardines, as money is no value to them at all. We had another talk with them. This time her husband was there so we got a lot of cider given to us, which we were very thankful for as it had been a very hot dry day. The fellows had rides on the donkey and horse, which they had there, thoroughly enjoying themselves. The following days we watched them reaping the corn in the fields around our harbour. They are very backward in machinery and ways of working to us.

On Sunday August 13th we were told that we were moving again to a place we had been before, known very well to us as the Caen sector. We left that sunny afternoon at 4.30 p.m. which was very hot. The roads were very dusty and as I was travelling in the back of a lorry I got very dirty and thirsty. We went through many ruined villages but one, which was Villers Bacage, I will never forget, as the damage done by our bombers was terrific. The craters were very large and in great numbers. Not a square yard was left untouched around the whole place. We arrived at our new harbour called Feugueralles. Here we started the old cry of us all, digging trenches. Still we have found them very useful in the past, so we haven't forgotten that fact. It was very close in the night, so we were pestered with gnats, which raised our arms, faces and legs to be covered in little bumps, which we couldn't help scratching. Jerry came over dropping flares and a few small bombs, as our bombers had been going over all day bombing him. So he spared a few planes to worry us as he thought.

The following days were very hot so the flies increased in numbers, which kept us busy trying to keep them away from the food and swill trench.

On Tuesday 15th we were taken in a lorry to see an "Ensa" show a few miles back. Here we saw for the first time some English girls, so the show was very interesting to the lads. It was great to be able to see a show over here with the guns rumbling in the distance and also that we were so near to the front yet not interfered by Jerries planes of which we haven't seen much of. As we sat waiting for the show to start we could see Caen in the distance, a town of big buildings and towers, which can be seen for miles around.

During the war we were so pleased to be entertained at concerts put on by ENSA (Entertainments National Service Association) who did a great job keeping our morale high. Some of the artists were serving in the Army and some came over from England and on one occasion we were lucky enough to see Vera Lynn, known as 'the Forces Sweetheart.' ENSA did a great job entertaining the troops when they could throughout the war; it was a great link with home. Many of the artists became famous after the war and in addition to Vera Lynn there were performers such as Tommy Trinder, Arthur Askey and Jimmy Edwards. As well as the letters we got from home we were kept more or less up to date with the way the war was going by the Regimental News Sheet called 'The Tamashanta.' I don't know how much of what was printed in it was propaganda to keep our spirits high but it was nice to get it every few weeks.

The following day, which was Wednesday 16th we were told that we were moving to another harbour near a village called St. Laurent. That night 2 Platoon were heavily attacked by "Doodle Bugs", our nick name for mosquitoes and gnats, which bothered you so much that we had to sleep with our towels over our faces, but still we got stung.

The following day the platoon was on road maintenance. I stopped in the harbour doing odd jobs, which were going. The news is very good so everyone is in high spirits. The weather still being very hot doesn't help the fly situation as they got worse everyday.

On Sunday 20th August we were told that we were moving again at 7 p.m., which didn't please us at all, as it meant digging in late which we don't like when we are tired. The new harbour was called Villers Carnet. Our platoon was on road maintenance for several days. We had three days of heavy rain, which didn't please us at all as our "bivys" were put up rough and the rain made its way in.

In the afternoon of Tues 22nd Aug we went through Falaise to an "Ensa" show, which turned out to be very good. The damage in the town was terrible, nothing else but rubble and dust flying about all over the place, which makes things difficult for travelling. It was here that we were told about Paris, of the fighting which was taking place there.

Thursday 24th Aug, we moved to a temporary harbour just the other side of Falaise. We went to bed after digging a small trench.

We rose early next morning to move on a long journey of roughly 60 miles, which was very interesting as Jerry had left so much material behind in his haste to get away from our boys. We came into a town called Beaumont Le Roger. In the centre of the town Jerry had blown a bridge, which the main road went over, so as we were the first troops in the town we had to bridge it. So we were well welcomed by the French people who gave us flowers and cider, which they drink more than we drink tea. We got talking to some of them and they took our photographs, so I am hoping they send a negative to home, as I gave them my address. We stopped in the town until 2.30 a.m. Here we left after taking some Jerry trailers with us to carry our surplus kit, which we have.

We moved again the following morning at 12.30 to a place called Ecardenville, which was very quiet.

On Sunday 27th August, we moved again at 5.30 p.m. for another ride in the trucks passing through towns and villages, who were very pleased to see us. We arrived safely to place called Fontaine Bellenger, near the big town of Louviers. The people here had many flags out for us. Also, they threw flowers and kisses to us, so we felt very proud as it showed their appreciation. The village folk came to see us and brought wine, pears, peaches and apples, so we enjoyed their company very much. That night it rained very heavily, so we were very glad of our bivies, which were put up very roughly, so the rain found its way in a little.

The platoon on Monday went out to clear the road of Tiger tanks, which had been knocked out. They found many mines, so the R.E.M.E moved the tank off the road. So it was then that a terrible accident happened killing our officer Lt. Baron, a very nice and well liked officer. It was a great blow to the platoon. The cause was found out to be two mines buried beneath the tank, so that they would go off if touched, which the lorries front wheel did. The mine detector won't detect if there is a bulk of metal near, so the mines were over-looked by the sweepers.

Clearing mines was a big part of my job and although it was dangerous I had been well trained and quickly gained experience. If we suspected there were mines laid on the route we wanted to take it was my job, together with others who had been trained, to go ahead of the Unit, check for mines and deactivate them. There were various types of mines including 'shoe mines' which were made of wood, had metal inside and were capable of killing a soldier or at least blowing his limbs off. I carried a heavy radio set on my back and would crawl on my hands and knees holding a detector in order to locate the mine. We would then mark a safe route with lengths of wire for those following. The lads had to keep to the safe path and not step over the wire. Unfortunately on December 23rd a good mate who was well liked, Paddy Lambert had his leg blown off as he stepped over the wire; he did survive thank goodness.

On Tuesday we moved again to the other side of the Seine, to a place called Muids, where there were some very nice people. Some of them, able to speak English, which we found very comforting. They told us that the Jerries are very wicked soldiers as they take everything without asking. There is one thing that struck me very funny and that was one of our fellows asked the farmer for some straw for his bed but he came to us first to ask our permission to give his own corn away. So that shows how the Germans really treat the people. That night we had a very nice nights sleep on straw in the barn, so we were very much relieved not having to dig in like we have been doing at other harbours.

On Wednesday 30th our platoon was on maintenance of the bridge across the river Seine, a wide and slow flowing river. It was at this town we had plenty of eggs, so our meals went down well.
On Thurs I decided to do my washing but the French people done it for me, so that saved me the job.

We moved again on Sat 2nd Sept for a long ride a distance of 50 miles. We arrived at a place called Gournay, a small but very nice place.

We were allowed out, so away we went to find the people very kind and excited. We went into a café and had Champagne, Red wine, Cognac and Cider, so we had a very good evening.

Sunday being the 3rd Sept marks the spot of 5 years of war so our thoughts were well ahead for the future.

On Monday 4th Sept we moved again to a farm half way to Picquiny, a very nice town. As we had some road maintenance to do, we had boiled eggs for tea, which were delicious. We arrived at Picquiny just to say for the night, as we were moving next day to a place called St. Pol. We all had bad eyes owing to the dust, as it contained lime so it was agony to try and sleep.

We rose early the next morning, Tuesday 5th Sept for another long ride by, passing Amiens a large well built City of churches and historical places. It looked very fine from the distance. We arrived at our new harbour near a big town called St. Pol. Here for once we slept on the deck, as digging in was unnecessary owing to Jerry retreating very quickly. We were advancing so fast that our supplies such as bread and Naafi rations couldn't keep up with us, so we found ourselves on hard tack or a simple form known to the troops as "Compo". The wind and rain made things very difficult to put up our bivies, which is our home for the time being.

On Wed 6th Sept we moved again, for another long journey roughly 80 miles. We past through many towns and villages, where the people had flags out for us and they were standing all along the roads for miles, waving and shouting. So we enjoyed the ride very much. We were also given the following articles, which were thrown or given to us when we stopped:- pears, apples, cigars, plums, also bottles of beer. We went through one big town called Lens a very big mining town as we could see the slag heaps from a long way off. The people lined the streets here 3 or 4 deep, so we were very happy as we have never seen such a sight like that before.
(The Official Record of this incident relates that the Company's move to Bellenghem near Courtrai was greatly hampered by cheering crowds which resulted in very slow progress.)

Thursday night, I was out on a recce for a bridge site. Here again we had plenty of things given to us as we went into places that British troops had not been into yet. Next day we stayed at the bridge near a place called Moen, a town of 4,000 people and only 36 Mackis to patrol at night times. The house we harboured at was a very nice place, as he had been a well to do man in the timber trade. So I was very interested in his machines, which he showed us without any bother. The woman of the house came out and gave us bunches of grapes, which were very nice indeed. I saw for the first time growing and that was tobacco, so I made a cigar with the help of the owner, it was very nice but strong as all cigars are.

Friday 8th Sept we moved at 5.30pm to a place called Audenaade, a very nice clean place better than the ones in France, as we are now in Belgium. Sat night I was out again on another recce for roads and bridges so we got a lovely welcome from the people that we past.

Sunday we moved again near a place called Mecfill. Here we were allowed out, so I put up my bivy and made my bed, washed and shaved and out I went for a stroll of 1 kilometre down the road to the village. I went to a dance there, the first one the people have had for four years, so we got a great welcome and the people couldn't do enough for us, so I enjoyed myself very much as it was a great change for me. I had a programme and 10 cigars given me, so I am keeping them for a souvenir. I came back that night to a lovely sleep in my little bivy a place we all make our home.

Monday morning was lovely and sunny, so our four engined bombers were going over to bomb Jerry. In the evening I stayed in as I was out the evening before, so I was in bed early for once.

Next morning Tuesday 12th we moved at 12.30 p.m. to a place this side of the Albert Canal, a wide and deep, slow flowing, so it was alright for a folding boat bridge, which we put across under occasionally mortar fire, but no one got hurt. In the evening we were allowed out, so I went down to the small village. I visited many little dance places without success as the music is very poor, so on the way back we heard a piano playing some well known tunes. So we entered to find an officer playing away and the people very happy, singing at the tops of their voices, so we stayed and enjoyed the evening very much.

The following morning we moved nearer the bridge, as we had to maintain it through the night. The evening came and we found that Jerry was *dropping flares looking for the bridge but he was a long way from it, much to our delight, as it had been hit once by a mortar bomb, causing a lot of hard work and time.*

We moved again on Thursday at 6 p.m. across the canal and through the town of Gheel. A town, that had been badly knocked about, as Jerry tried to make a stand there but failed.

Today Friday 15th we heard that Lt. Murray, Sgt. Harris and two other sappers got wounded through a shell which landed near their platoon harbour, which is 1 platoon. Our guns have been firing heavily all night long and occasionally through the day, so we have got to get used to them again as we have been so far behind the lines to hear them. We started building a body for the trailer, which we found, left behind by Jerry in his mad rush to get away.

As they retreated the German Army left a large amount of equipment behind a lot of which they demolished and smashed up. However, as the allies drove them back to Germany in full retreat they just abandoned equipment and vehicles which we were then able to repair and make good use of.

Gerry aged about 12 on holiday with his mother in Exmouth.

Gerry's father with his British Railways lorry of which he was so proud.

Gerry, aged 16 years, in Worthing Home Guard.

The Home Guard badge.

Regimental badge and shoulder flashes for 15th Scottish Division.

Basic training in 1943 – note the 15th Scottish shoulder flash.

Part of Gerry's original uniform from the
Royal Engineers -15th Scottish Division.

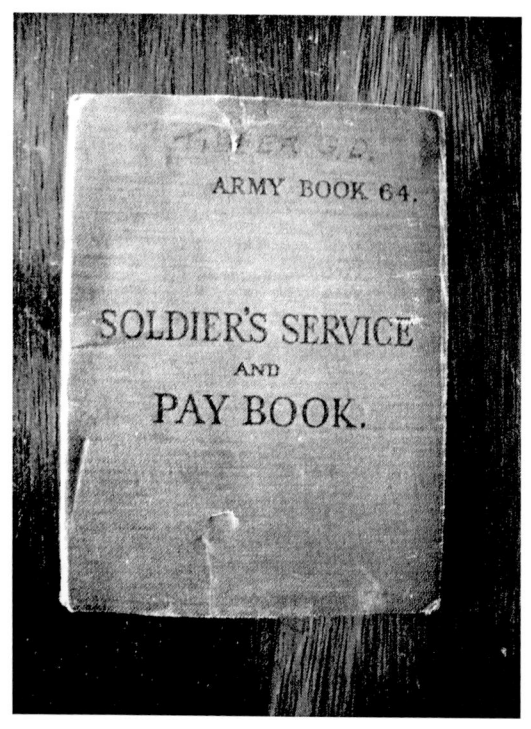

Gerry's Service Pay Book.

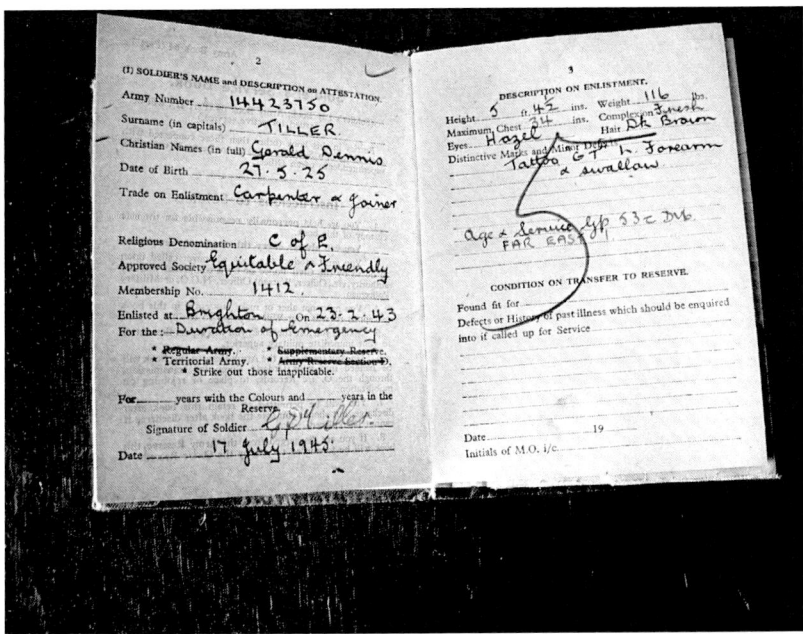

An entry from the Pay Book.

Training note book issued to Gerry during his basic training.

Notes made by Gerry during his training giving details of enemy mines and how to defuse them

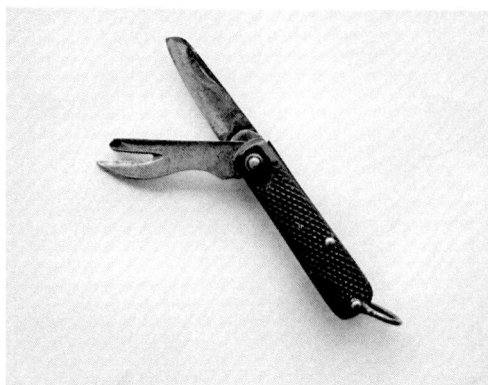

Army-issue knife.

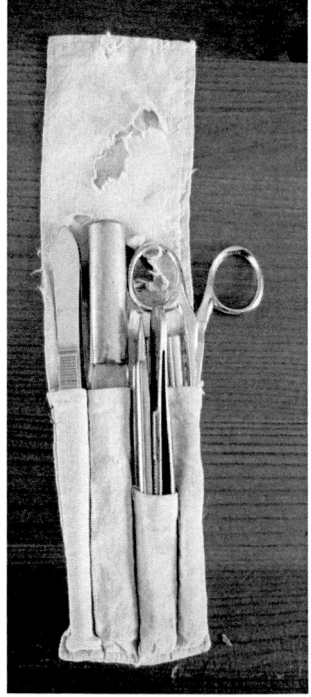

First Aid kit used by Gerry throughout the war.

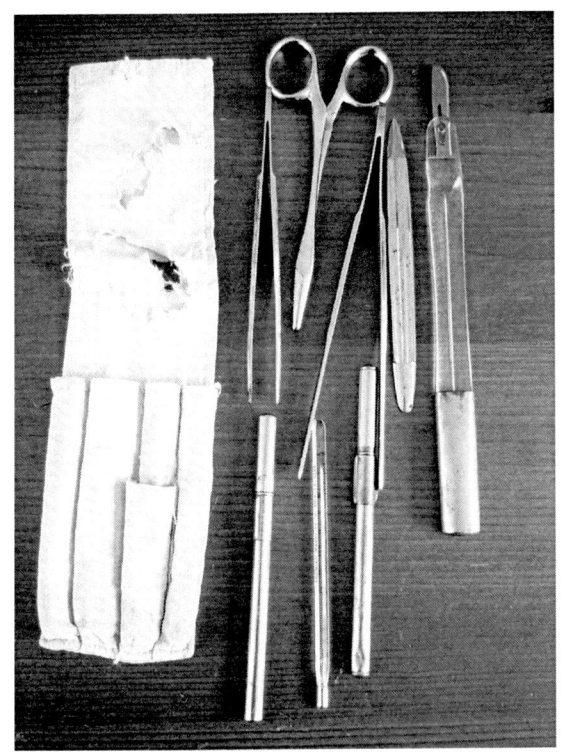

First Aid kit. Note the scalpel made by Gerry and used by him to remove shrapnel from injured colleagues.

The pen used by Gerry to write the diary.

The exercise books in which Gerry
transcribed in detail the entries
from the small diaries.

The original small diaries which Gerry kept
hidden at the bottom of his tool box.

"Tommy V Bosch" — 2 Platoon
"Normandy"   278 Field Coy. RE. 90
                  B.L.A.
            (Started writing) 31st July 44.

It was on Friday 16th June that we left Wanstead Flats for Royal Albert docks, we sailed at 6 p.m. for an unknown destination which is now known to us as France.

The Thames was calm and very busy with other troop ships bound for the open seas, our ship which was a "Yanky" one was called "George Durant", the crew 73 of them were very ~~sociablt~~ sociable and jolly, we enjoyed the trip down the Thames to the Estuary, we anchored there for forming up as we couldn't go through the Straits unless under cover of darkness owing to Jerries observation.

The passage through was very rough so we couldn't get a lot of sleep, we rose next morning to find us anchored of Beachy Head, it was a lovely fresh sunny morning of June 18th, the

The first page of the diary.

The first entry in the diary.

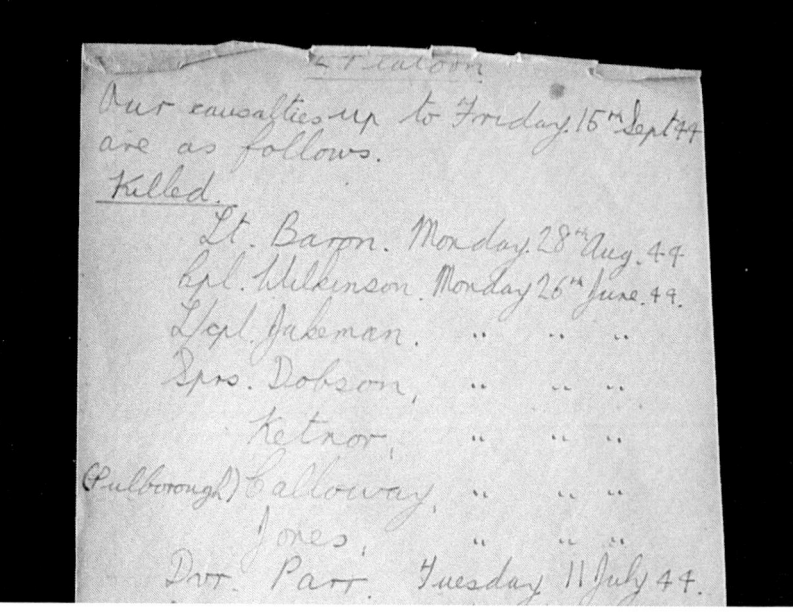

Notes recorded by Gerry of his colleagues who were killed and injured. He stopped making these lists as there were so many of his friends who died.

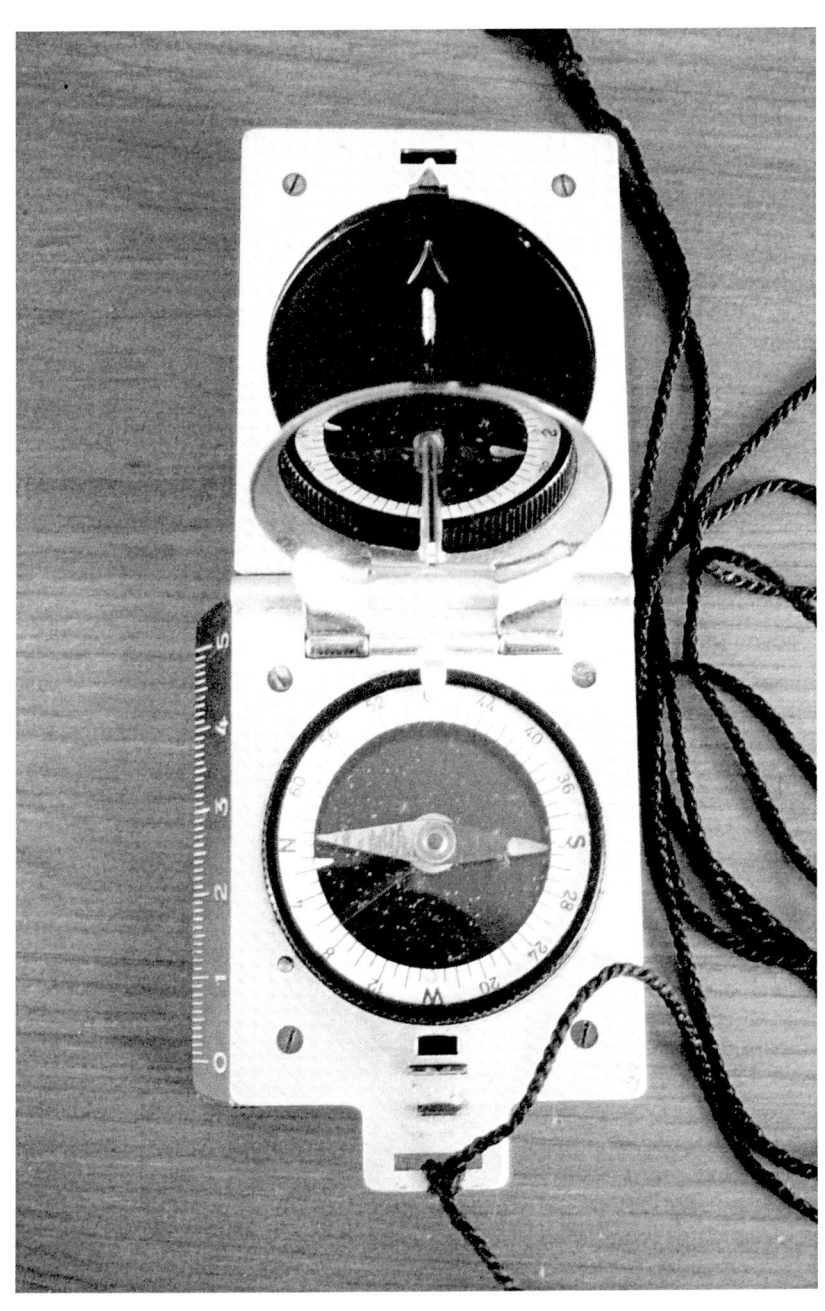

Compass given to Gerry by captured German Officer.

German bank notes, which were worthless, and found by Gerry in a bank that had been bombed by the British.

Also found a 500,000,000 (five-hundred million) marks bank note issued in 1923 during the recession in Germany.

Regimental plaque made by Gerry from a German shell case. He flattened the case, cut it to shape and had it engraved by a German jeweller. The names depicted are of rivers crossed and towns captured and liberated by the 15th Scottish during the war.

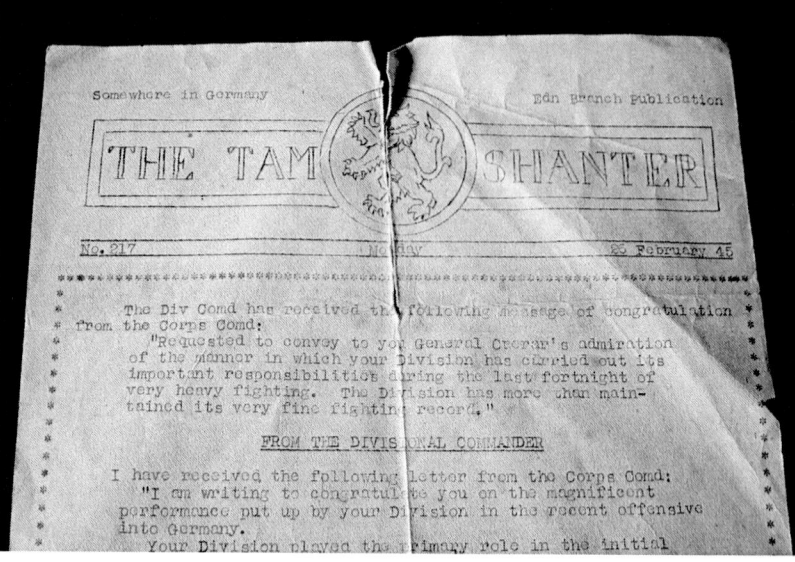

The 'Tam O'Shanter'. This was circulated by the Regiment throughout the war to keep the troops up to date with war and home news.

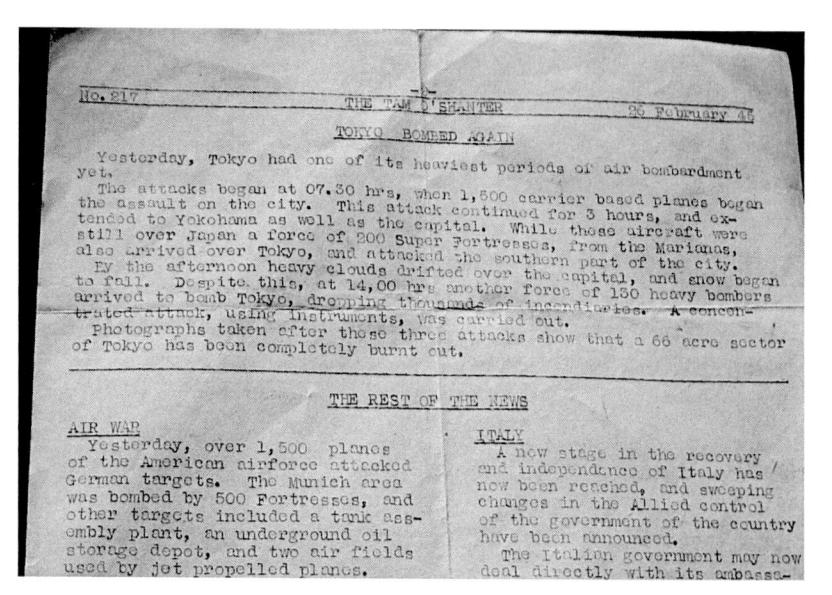

The Tam O'Shanter also kept the troops informed about what was happening in other theatres of war.

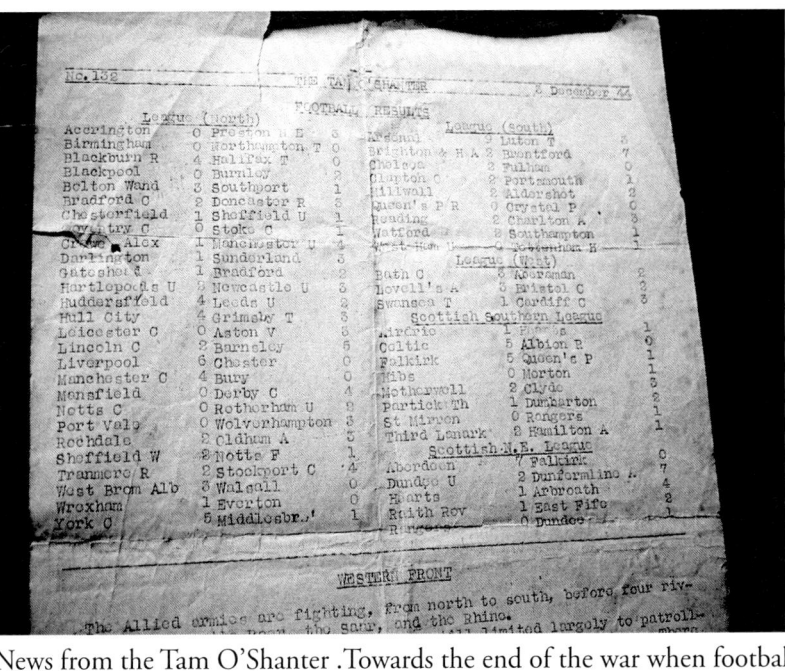

News from the Tam O'Shanter. Towards the end of the war when football was being played back home the troops were kept up to date with the results – happiness for some, not so good news for others perhaps.

Belgium, Holland and Germany

On Sat 16th Sept we went out during the evening to the bridge site over the Escaut Canal. A place where Jerry put up a very stiff fight, as he had doped his men and they were yelling and dancing about as if they were drunk. The main Jerry had been heavily mortared all day long, so were going to take over that night but 279 Field boy R.E. did instead, much to our relieve as the mortar fire was deadly at the time. We came back to the billet harbour to a good nights sleep.

Next morning Sunday at 8.30 we went to the Escaut Canal to take over for 24 hrs. Well, Jerry shelled and mortared the place all day long, as we were taking infantry and wounded to and fro by assault boats, which were pulled across by ropes. We took many Jerry prisoners and wounded across, all very young and worn out. They gazed up in the sky to see our fighters and transports taking parachutist to the Rhine area. It was off these prisoners that I got a pair of wings and a small badge. They stare at you very bland and miserable look on their faces, as they couldn't make out what why we were so happy and bright, while all the mortar and shells were dropping around. We also took across men, women and children with babies only a few months old, yet they never flinched and shook hands with us and patted us on the back. We got praises from all who went across, saying that we were doing a grand job in difficult conditions, which we were having at the time. During the day Sgt. Major Dunsmuir got slightly wounded in the back and one arm, so he was rushed away to the R.A.M.C. down the road. Also, Sgt. Greenaway was badly shocked by blast but he only went away for a short rest and is now back in his platoon, carrying on the good work, owing to our officer being killed in the past weeks. As nightfall came we were troubled with a lonely sniper in a building that had been well blasted by our artillery. Every time we went across he would fire two or three rounds of tracer at us, but we were not scared in a way as he was a bad shot. He was later sorted by one lonely Vickers gun, which I think he didn't appreciate, as he didn't fire anymore. We were all tired and badly shaking so we made great haste next morning Monday, to get back as we had a very busy and tiring night. Still we done the job without casualties in the platoon, which was very surprising. I went to bed as soon as we got back and slept till 2.30, then I arose to find a letter from home and my paper, so I laid in bed and read my letter with interest.

The following days we were given some Jerry rations, also some sweets, which were captured by our advancing Armies. On Thursday morning at 8.30 we moved again for a journey of 40 miles into Holland, to a place called Eindhoven. We crossed the border at 1.30. We found the people very nervous, as the Germans had treated them badly. They had to stand to attention by the road if any German convoy went past. The Germans also looted many things from them before they departed. They like us British tommies as they say we are kind hearted and gentle. That night I was on guard for 3 hrs 50 mins, a long and weary time, as Jerry wasn't far away, so it made us keep wide awake in case anything should come our way. During the day our big transport planes "Dakotas" were going over dropping supplies and men beyond the Rhine. We saw one of our planes crash in flames not far away from us, two men bailed out.

On 17th September and the following days Operation Market Garden took place. We saw hundreds of our aircraft, mainly Dakotas, fly over carrying troops who parachuted into areas around Arnhem. The plan was to take eight bridges on the German/Dutch border at Arnhem, Eindhoven and Nijmegen. It is accepted that a lot of mistakes were made during that Operation. It is now believed that intelligence was not communicated, misinterpreted or ignored and as a result allied troops suffered very heavy losses. After the war stories of many brave acts of heroism were reported when the soldiers were attempting to capture the bridges – a very good film called 'A Bridge Too Far' was later made telling the story. Although I didn't take part directly in that action I have very good reason to remember it because something happened which affected me greatly at the time and still does to this day. I did not write about it in my Diary for obvious reasons.

A few days after 17th September an Officer told me and several mates that we had to go with him on a special mission. He took us to a wooded area and, although he had told us what our task was, the sight that met our eyes was horrific and unimaginable! Hanging in the branches of the trees were the bodies of airborne soldiers still attached to their parachutes, others were lying dead on the ground. There were approximately 100 to150 I am not sure exactly how many, but they had evidently been dropped from the planes in the wrong place and shot by the Germans as they came down. Our task was to cut them out of the trees and bury them. However, when some of the Artillery lads who were with us started to cut the trees down, a lot of the automatic weapons the bodies were still holding would go off. They obviously had the safety catches 'off' ready for action when they had jumped and so it was first necessary for us to ensure that their automatic weapons were safe. Some of the lads went to a nearby farmhouse and got ladders. They then climbed into the trees and made sure the safety catches were 'on' on the guns. We had to climb up and cut the poor lads out of their parachutes and lower them down out of the branches. I actually cut a piece off a parachute from a poor lad I had got out of the trees and I have kept it to this day in memory of him. At the time I think I thought I could get the poor lad's I.D papers and maybe, after the war, send the piece of his parachute to his loved ones in memory of him; that of course was not possible. When I look at it and touch it today I shed tears, but I think it is important I don't forget those poor lads.

The next duty was to bury them, which was very traumatic because rigor mortice had set in with most of them making their bodies stiff. We used a bulldozer to dig a mass grave and, as I was a carpenter, I got some wood and made a number of small crosses and put the names of the dead soldiers on them. The Officers with us recorded their personal details. It was very distressing and after burying about 50 of my comrades I just couldn't carry on. I was so upset and I asked the Officer if I could be excused. He agreed and I returned to my Unit where I had several hours rest. Some of my mates were affected the same.

We were given strict instructions not to talk about the incident and so of course I did not record it in my Diary. I believe that the facts were kept secret for many years after the war but I have never forgotten the events of that day and it still upsets me to think about it. I often wonder if the loved ones of those poor soldiers ever knew what happened to them. There are no records of this event in the Official War Records of 278 but it is now a well known fact that many airborne troops were dropped in the wrong place behind enemy lines during Operation Market Garden. Many died.

The platoon moved through Eindhoven to do maintenance on a bridge across the river, which was occasionally shelled by Jerry. On Sat. evening "Dakotas" towing gliders went over in great force for about 3 or 4 hours. The Dutch people were amazed at the sight, wondering where all the planes had come from, as England is such a small country to them.

During the following days we went to the pictures and shows in Eindhoven. On Wed morning at 7.30 a.m. we moved to a place 9 miles from the town, so we still went to shows there which we found a great change. All day I worked on building the trailer as we had the time and timber to make a good job, so our progress was fast.

The platoon were working on the cross roads, as the tanks had made big ruts which they filled in without any trouble. That evening Jerry started sending a few shells over, hitting a Scout car, setting it on fire. We that's H.Q. were on guard for 3 nights running, as the lads were on the roads and bridges, which needed attention all the time.

On Friday 29th Sept we went into Eindhoven to a show but it was cancelled, so we had a good look round the shops, buying one or two things, which interested us.

On Sat 30th we worked all day long on the trucks, which badly needed maintenance, so the day went quickly as our minds were occupied.

Sunday morning we were aroused early by Jerry shells, which dropped in the field close to us, so we made quick haste for our trenches. The Artillery in the field were shaken up a bit but nobody hurt thank goodness. Also that day we had 20 cigars each, so everywhere was smelling very sweet.

On Tuesday Oct 3rd we moved to a place called Helmond, about 11 miles from Eindhoven, so we were often in the town during the evening.

The following days I was in and out of Eindhoven, so I had a good look round of the place.

On Sat 7th we were bridging all day on the canal. One pontoon got punctured, so it began to sink quickly owing to the weight of the half-track. So we made great haste to the far bank as it was nearest. Luckily the bank wasn't steep so the vehicle was able to get on the road without any trouble. The lads got wet but their clothes soon dried near a fire back at camp.
Sunday morning I went down to the site to guard the equipment. So I had many rides in the boats up and down the canal, which was very enjoyable. On Monday 9th the G.O.C. of the division came to congratulate us on our very good calm work, at the Escaut Canal near Gheel, where our platoon

were ferrying. He said that owing to our good work the operation was completed. After this proud address we were given the day off. I went to Eindhoven again and had a very good time. On arriving back I saw our new officer Lt. Niven, also other ranks to make our platoon strength up.

Wednesday I went into town and went to a person's house and had supper. A very nice, enjoyable evening.

On Friday 13th the town was all excited because a car containing the King, Monty and Eisenhower passed through the streets, a great surprise for everyone.

On Monday 16th I went to the town to the friends house and obtained by a little bargaining, a torch made by Philips which doesn't need any batteries, so I find it very handy.

Tuesday I went to the pictures and saw "Gentleman Jim" a very nice picture, so I was glad I went. We returned to sit by the fire talking about different things that had happened to us in the past years.
The following days we wrote letters or went out in the afternoon to Eindhoven, a place we know well by now, as we have visited the place so often.

Apart from my diary I wrote many letters home to my family and friends during the war. In fact some of my mates used to 'take the mickey' out of me about it. Of course I knew that all my letters would be censured for security reasons and we were not allowed to tell anyone about where we were in Europe. However that didn't stop me!

When I lived at home with my parents I used to play darts with my Dad and when I left to go to war he took the dartboard off the wall and replaced it with a big map of Europe.
While I was in training an officer told me about a secret code I could use when writing letters that would tell my folks back home where I was. He swore me to secrecy and I never told anyone else about it. It worked like this.
 My parents had a dog and cat at home called 'Dopey' and 'Whiskey.' Every time I sent a letter home I would end it with the words 'Give Dopey and Whiskey a big kiss from me.' That was a code to my parents to look

two or three sentences back in the letter. Now suppose I was in Caen in France, I would put a very small dot in the middle of a letter C which appeared in a word I had written two or three sentences from the end. I would also put a dot in the letter A when it next appeared. Likewise with the letters E and N. My Dad would then work out that I was somewhere near the town of Caen and he would mark it on the map of Europe he had on the wall. I did this right through the war and by doing so my parents followed my progress across France, Belgium, Holland and Germany. It was not the greatest secret code that was used during World War II and I guess the experts at Bletchley Park would have soon cracked it, but thanks to Dopey and Whiskey it worked for us!

On Sat 21 Oct I was asked to attend a lecture by a war official at a nearby town, on the subject everyone at the present is very interested in and that is demobilisation scheme. So we left that morning at 10.30 for a short ride with other fellows and N.C.O's of the company. It was held at a College, a very nice place. Those that attended were from Sappers upwards, so the opinions, which were raised were good ones.
Sunday our football team played the civvies of Helmond, a very good fast game. The score was three all.

Monday I helped to put a new roof on the officers truck, as the rain had found its way through the other one. The lads were on the new mine detectors, so I was glad, as those things get very boring if used for any length of time.

Tuesday we moved at 5.30 p.m. to the other side of Eindhoven, just for the night. I was wakened at 4.30 a.m. to go on a recce. It was a very cold morning, so I found my gloves and overcoat very welcome. We met up with the Recce Corp and moved forward to find enemy opposition, which we didn't know. It was misty, so clear vision was difficult. We went through a village and what a welcome we got, as we were the first Tommies they had seen. They told us many handy positions of Jerry, so we crawled along very slow, very keened up or nervous, as I should say. All of sudden two Jerry anti tank guns opened up on us at 200 yds range but owing to the thick mist they missed the leading truck, so we hastily retreat to a small farm way back on the same road. Here we stayed for a few hours while our mortars sent over a few shells to try and drive them out of it. It was then when a civvy on a cycle rode up and told us that there were twenty Jerries up the road on patrol, so we took up positions for defence. They came to some haystacks to our front at 75 yards, so the "besa" had a nice target. They laid quiet for a while, so we sent back by radio for more recce cars but they couldn't reach us owing to us being cut off for 3 hrs now. So a word came through that two Churchill tanks were on their way up to break through the small patrol, which they did much to our relief. We continued on our journey with the support of tanks and came to a bridge, which had been destroyed by Jerry, so we measured the gap in amidst of cheering people, who were very happy to see us. We had dinner of fried eggs and bread. So we went on after the small "Scissor" bridge carried by a tank had been put across, to a place called Dendonk, which was heavily defended by Jerry so we couldn't get through to measure the blown bridge. Our infantry went in to the attack and fought all that night and were very tired in the morning.

We slept that night very soundly as we were tired. We moved that morning Thursday 26th Oct to a place near Tilburg, which was still held in places.

Friday morning I was out on another recce for a bridge, which was still under fire at intervals. We crept up at the backs of houses ducking down now and again to get out of the way of mortar shells.

Sat morning we went up there again, as an attack had been put over and we could hear the people cheering the infantry as they went through. On the other side of the canal was a big fire in a tar factory. The film unit men were there and they took shots of me standing at the edge of the blown bridge, also of the infantry going across the canal in assault boats. We slept that night in civvy billets after working hard all day on a Bailey bridge. A "double double" 120 feet, a very fine piece of work done in a very short time.

It was Sunday, we were up early to move again to a place near Derne. Then we saw a doodle bug go over heading for England. We were billeted in some woods, so the fire was the best place during the day and the bed at night. We were out again on a recce for a minefield but we couldn't get to it, owing to heavy fire, so we return and waited till it was clear. Then returned one evening to clear the mines but not one mine located, so we were glad, as they are difficult things to handle with, in cold weather. Owing to being late that night we layed in bed. Then my parcel came, so I got up to see the useful contents, which Mother had sent.

Thursday 2nd Nov. I was on guard that evening so we were able to see the barrage put up by the Siegfried Line against our bombers, which were going over in great force, so our time went quick much to our delight. We moved the following morning to the other side of Derne, to a farm building, which was very welcomed, as the weather has turned very cold.

Sat Nov 4th, I was informed that I was one of the two going for a 48hrs leave to Brussels, so I was very excited as reports coming from others which have been, told me that I was in for a nice time. Well I dashed around getting my new suit out and cleaning my very neglected boots. I slept sound that night to rise at 6 a.m. I hastily dressed and had my breakfast. Then we were taken by half-track down to Helmond to the R.A.S.C who were taking us by road. A very long cold journey but it did not bother us, as we knew that we were to sleep in civvy beds for two nights. We arrived at the great City at 1.30 pm. We done all the writing and filling in which was annoying at the time. Well we got our key to our room, which was on the 6th floor so we took the lift to save the long drag of the stairs, which I walked once. We hastily washed, shaved and had our tea, which we were ready for. Then out we went to a very good variety show at the A.B.C. theatre. We enjoyed it very much, as it was such a change to see a show among the civvies. We came out after the show and had a drink in a very modern public house, after which we retired to a soft bed for a sound nights sleep. We were wakened at 7 p.m., by a waiter with a nice sweet cup of tea, which went down very well. The meals during our stay were of the first class cooking, so I enjoyed them every day. The rest of the time we spent looking round the City and riding on the tramcars, which were free for all troops on leave there. I enjoyed every moment of it, so anyone going there it is just a life of luxury. We left to come back at 2 p.m. a distance of 150 kilometres, 5 hrs ride in a vehicle. The following days I spent in the harbour getting over the lovely time that I have had.

Throughout the war, particularly when we were up at the front and engaging with the enemy, we would spend about ten days in combat usually living in very basic and uncomfortable conditions and with little sleep. We were then relieved and went back behind our lines for some well needed rest and recuperation. Sometimes we were lucky enough to be allowed to spend a couple of days in nearby towns or cities such as Brussels or Eindhoven. When we went to those places we all went a bit mad as you would expect of young lads who had experienced terrible frightening things. We knew we were going back to the front and could be killed any day. We went to the cinema to watch a film and get our minds' off war, we went to bars and got very drunk and we went to the local brothels. Because I was a qualified First Aider- I'm not sure what that had to do with it though- I was officially given a supply of condoms which we called 'johnnies' to dish out to the lads. Judging by the number some of them asked for I envied their stamina!

We were always made very welcome by the locals who we had liberated from the German occupation and we would often be invited to their homes for meals. Those visits provided a very nice break from the traumas of war.

On Sat 18th Nov I went out on a recce to look for some trees, which were strewn across the road. This road was under observation by Jerry so it was difficult for us to see the actual job, which was to be done, as he would send occasional shells over to stop our progress. In the evening of the same day we were out with one section to clear these trees in our path. This we did right up to the small canal where the bridge was blown. It was a very weary job as it was so dark and quiet which made things worse.

Next day Sunday 19th Nov we were out on the same road clearing it of debris, filling in craters and removing odd mines, which he had laid in haste. While we were working a nearby house exploded, surprising all of us. It was found to be a bobby trap set by Jerry on a bedroom door, which was pushed open by two infantrymen and 1 sapper belonging to the Company. The two infantrymen escaped with slight injuries and shock but the poor sapper was killed. So we learnt another lesson by some ones downfall.

On Monday 20th we moved that morning at 10.30 a.m. to a place called Liesiel, a town which had taken a terrible blow of shells and bombs. That night the lads were out working all night. So as usual H.Q. supplied the guard a very cold and wet night, still we were not green as we have done guards before.
On Wed 22nd we moved again in the morning to the other side of the canal. To a civvy house, which was leaking badly owing to the slates being blown or smashed by shrapnel. So a Cpl. and myself found some spare tiles

in the attic. So finding a ladder we climbed to the work that lay ahead. We worked away all day and completed the roof to our satisfaction. We also got a bigger stove for the kitchen from a nearby house. We lit the fire as the lads were coming in wet from the drizzling rain and wind, which had been on all day making the roads and paths very muddy. We settled down well for the night with the old wireless going strong on newly charged batteries.

The next morning we were wakened at 7.30 to find only that we were to move again after all our work the previous day, still that's the army and nothing could alter the fact. It was Friday 24th and our officer called the Sgt and me to be briefed for a recce for a bridge near Venray, which was under shellfire, so our journey, was a risky one. Still it had to be done so we set of with high spirits and faith of our return. It was a fine, but a cold wind was blowing. We arrived at the bridge site and done the necessary, such as mines etc. The section, which was with us, started clearing the bank seats. We hadn't been working long when over came the shells all around the two vehicles which were standing on the road. We hastily dived for the trenches, which contained water but we didn't think of the cold at all. So we were wet when it was all over with. Then it started to rain so we made way back to collect our waterproofs. Then we heard some more coming over, so we went into the house only to find Lt. Niven and Dvr. Pickwell injured by shrapnel. The officer was feeling pretty groggy, as he was hit between the shoulders and the wound was not bleeding, also his arm was numb. The driver was hit in the left arm at the muscle, so he was bleeding heavily. After the shelling had finished they were rushed to a A.D.S. in Venray. We stopped in the house for two or three hours as it had shaken us up seeing those injured so quickly. We continued later in the day without being annoyed again, so we were able to complete the job of the bank seats.

On Sunday 26th we moved again to a new harbour near Horst, where we were bridging all day but was finished early so bed was the first call on arriving back. Rum was issued that night, so it went down very well, as it is very wet under foot in this country of Holland.

Tuesday 28th we stayed in all day, some doing a little washing, others like myself frying eggs and chips in butter which we had saved from previous meals. We filled ourselves well but still ate our dinner at 5.30 p.m.

Then I wrote 8 letters much surprise to the lads as they say I need a typewriter not a pen.
We moved on Wed 29th Nov. to a new harbour outside Venray, a town on the way to Venlo.

On Sat 2nd Dec. a big barrage by our Artillery for a big push in direction on Venlo. Not many injured and the operation went well.

On Sunday 3rd Dec I listened to the King speaking in London on the Home Guard standing down. I listened with interest as once I was in it, so what the King said concerned me.

The following days I came over queer, also I had a big boil on my neck, which I treated daily. It was very painful, so I couldn't do much in the way of work.

On Thursday 7th Dec we moved to Asten for 7 days in civvy billets much to our delight, as we all had colds and other such common complaints. I found on moving that some kind person had taken my Wellington boots, so I was very annoyed as it meant me having wet feet some time to come.

The following days we spent in so called Heaven to us fellows, as in the past had been fairly rough living. The people were very good to us, looking after us like relations. We went on liberty trucks to Eindhoven and not forgetting Helmond, places where the lads have had a many good time in the past, so those places were worth going back too. Our platoon officer Lt. Niven came back to carry on with the managing which the platoon needed. All of us excited because we hear that we were getting leave for the New Year, so every one was on their toes.

On Sunday 17th Dec we moved at 8.15 from those lovely comfortable billets to go up the front at a place called Heijthuysen. On arriving there we noticed that Jerry was very active with his aircraft again, dropping bombs in odd places. The Ack-ack boys were firing all the time he was over so his journey was a rough and risky one.

On Tuesday the lads were out lifting "R" mines near our harbour. The compressor was used at it was thought that Jerry might have laid some "schu" mines there so we were not taking any chances.

The following days more mines were lifted without any injury. It had started to freeze very hard so our sleeping place, which was a barn roof, was very cold. So cold in fact that water froze within an hour.

It was drawing near Xmas and mail was coming in batches. I received a lovely parcel from girlfriend so it came in just right.

As we progressed through Holland, Belgium and Germany I occasionally received parcels from home which was great and any homemade food that my Mum sent was very welcome. The army food wasn't bad but often we had to make do with combat rations which were mainly dried or powdered and we just had to add water. When we ran out of food we would receive supplies dropped by parachute but we had to be careful retrieving them because snipers might try to take us out. However we always managed to add to our rations by various means. If we came across a farm we would often get fresh vegetables and eggs and sometimes, when the ground was frozen, we would dig up potatoes in the fields with our bayonets. We also found lorries that had been abandoned by the Germans, some containing frozen food.

One amusing incident happened that helped the lads out when I came across a biscuit factory near where we were billeted. Although the factory was working during the day my mate and I decided to break in at night. We climbed over the fence and broke in where we found dozens of boxes with foreign writing on the side. We took as many boxes as we could outside the factory where one of our mates, who was an interpreter, was waiting with a vehicle. We showed him our loot which we thought was biscuits but you can imagine our surprise when he told us that they were eggs! I don't know how many there were, it was hundreds. When an Officer saw all the lads in my platoon scoffing them he demanded to know where we got them from and I told him we had nicked them from a biscuit factory. He told me in no uncertain terms that what we had done was illegal, marched three mates and me to the cookhouse with the boxes of eggs and all ranks enjoyed them in some shape or form for quite a while! I remember one time when we were resting by the roadside I fried some eggs for the officers on the hot part of the engine of a tank! I was quite handy at that sort of thing and also showed the lads how to make a kind of butter out of milk by just shaking and shaking it. The war certainly taught me to be practical and inventive!

On Sat 23rd the lads were out on mine clearing but this time it was "schu" mines and the ground being very hard through frosts, the prodding method had to be used which is very slow this weather. Then a terrible thing happened Paddy Lambert trod on one, which blew his leg off just below the knee. He was rushed away to a hospital in Derne. Paddy was very well liked by all, for his joking and high spirited ways at all times, so he was missed very much by all. Another sad thing was that he was due to go on leave in January, so it was very bad luck on his part.

On Xmas Eve I was on guard and as we walked up and down the hard frozen pathway we thought and spoke of the things our friends and relations would be doing at that time. In the distance we could hear the guns going and in the sky were many bombers, as we could see their vapour trails against the bright moonlight sky.

Next morning was Xmas day and everyone was dressed in their best suits and singing many old favourites, which were being played on the wireless. We also listened to the many bells, which were being rung all over Blighty. So we listened with interest, as everyone was concerned. We had a very nice dinner, which was cooked at H.Q. We all had beer, sweets, cigars, cigarettes and many other small luxuries which only come at this time of the year.

The following days were very cold with bleak winds and as we were in a farm we felt the cold very much. Evenings I went to the pictures, which were held at the Convent not far from our billet.

Sunday 31st which was New Years Eve I had a few bottles of beer left from Xmas, so these were drunk just to celebrate a little. Some of the lads stayed up to see the New Year in but myself being cold and tired went to bed only to be wakened at midnight by a tin can being kicked about by the lads who said they were kicking the old year out.
1st January 1945. This day brought no great excitement. I went to H.Q. on a wireless course, while the others were working on the road, as it was very slippery so sand had to be laid for the safety of all who came our way.

On Wed 3rd Jan it started to thaw hard, which we had been looking for, as travelling was becoming difficult. I went to bed that night only to be wakened at midnight, to be told that we were going to Brussels on blackout work etc., at a Convent, which was to be a Div rest camp. The journey, which lay ahead was a long one, also very cold. We arrived at 8.30 at a place called Genval, which was 12 kilometres from Brussels. We had a meal then retired for a few hours sleep, which we were in need of. We moved to the other side of this big estate, which surrounded a large lake. This we understood was a holiday estate during summer periods, before the war. We had a very nice billet, so we soon settled in. It was still freezing hard and the lake was about three or four inches thick, so walking across it was quicker than going round. We went to Brussels for one evening and had a very good time, as I had a few francs in my wallet left from my leave there. The following days were spent sharpening tools and getting stores for the big job, which lay ahead. It was still snowing hard, which froze at night times, so a keen eye had to be kept on the transport, although anti freeze was installed. At hard frosts it will freeze as it contains a certain amount of water.

On Tuesday 9th we were sent to the Convent to start on the blackouts. I spent most of the day measuring and taking stores required for the job. We worked the following days on blacking out half of the windows, as far as the material went.

Then came Sat 13th which was a half-day for us to spend in Brussels. I had a good look round with the lads who hadn't been before. We had a good few drinks and visited the canteens, which were very welcomed.

On Tuesday 16th we moved to a place called La Hulpe, not much nearer to the city. Here we were put into civvy billets, which were very welcomed, as we all needed looking after these days. I took the clogs with me to work, as I knew I could get them painted. These I did in what I called our dinner hour. I slept in a nice soft cosy bed, which was difficult to get out of in the morning, as we had been used to sleeping on a hard floor, so it was a great change for us.
On Friday 19th Jan it started to thaw rapidly, so water and mud was very plentiful around this district. In the next few days it started to freeze hard again, so it was very dangerous to walk on the cobbled roads.

On Monday 29th Jan the temperature was 20 degrees below zero, the coldest day I ever had known.

Again on 1st Feb it thawed very fast and turned to rain, so it was a lot warmer.

On Friday 2nd Feb eight of us and a N.C.O. were left at Genval 3 miles from La Hulpe to finish of the remaining work, as the rest of the platoon had to return to the Division for future operations.

The remaining 8 days we worked hard all day long, trying to get it finished in time. I spent a very happy time at the Convent, at dances, which were run by the staff, so I tried my hand at dancing but made more of a fool of myself than anything else, still I enjoyed it so it didn't matter so much. I had my photo taken with the staff at the last dance they had there, as the club was being temporarily closed down because the central heating had burst.

On Monday 12th Feb we moved at 8.30 on a 3 tonner, with all our kit and tools for a long journey to somewhere in Germany, as a big push had been made and our Company were very busy on mines etc. The distance we covered that day was 140 miles, so we were in great need of a rest, which I spent in a dark cellar of a school, which had badly been knocked about by our artillery in the attack which took place, two or three days before hand.

We were now in Germany having liberated France, Belgium and Holland. I remember we felt proud of the way we were pushing the enemy back and most of the German local people we came across were pleased to see us. They looked very sad, tired and weary of war.

Then on Thursday 15th Feb we moved at 4.30 a.m. to a place called Cleve, a German town, which was partly under water, which the Jerries had done thinking it would slow up our advance but the Army overcome that by using "Ducks" a very handy little boat vehicle. We moved again after a day of looting, so everyone was full of different articles, such as biscuits, watches, money and all kinds of things. The water was rising fast. It was ankle deep, so we moved up to the hill where all the artillery were pounding away at Jerries defences. We arrived at some badly battered houses, which we made our homes for 3 or 4 days. We slept on mattresses which were very soft and all though the guns were going all night long, we slept very soundly.

While we were going through the town that day we came across a Bank that had been badly damaged. A few of us went in and found a room with thousands of German bank notes just lying on the floor and wet from the flooding. Some of the lads just threw them about, other jokers used them to wipe their backsides on but I kept mine and still have them. Amongst them is a Reich bank 1924 500 million marks note. I was told that because of the depressed state of the Germany economy between the wars the German money was devalued and the notes we found were worthless. As in any war looting is quite common but I can honestly say that I never took anything from houses or buildings that were the personal belongings of civilians. I did end up with several bits and pieces of memorabilia which I have kept. One thing that I do treasure is a hand compass that was given to me by a German Officer who was a prisoner of war. When he was captured and I searched him he gave it to me saying that he had no more use for it.

On Monday 19th Feb we were under 2 hrs notice to move, so I wrote letters, while others slept and read books to pass the time away.

Thursday 22nd Feb a big attack was put in by many Divisions, including ours. The barrage was terrific, our job was road maintenance, which was no bother at all, as the badly knocked about houses supplied plenty of rubble, which is very good material in our work, as it makes a nice solid surface for heavy traffic.

On Sat 24th Feb reveille was 4.30 a.m. This was because our company had a bridge to build over a site, which had been badly blown by Jerry in his hasty retreat. We worked hard all day long, under the terrific barrage, which was in aid of another big attack by another Division, which was going to relieve our Division from the line, as it had heavy casualties, as we had come up against Jerries artillery. The smoke from the shells bursting was choking, so we felt very tired and weary, as it had been a very long day for us. We finished the 100 ft Bailey at 8.30 p.m., so we returned to our billets near Cleve to a very good nights sleep, which we all were in great need of.

On Monday 26th Feb, another attack was put in, which was very successful, by the 3rd Division. Again a heavy barrage was sent over and many worn, tired and weary prisoners came through our lines, who passed us looking very sad. All were very young fellow of Hitlers youth movement.

Next day Generals and many officers came round speaking to us while we worked. We heard also that day that the King, Churchill and Monty were on our sector. Some of the lads saw them in a nearby village but myself I was unlucky.

On Wed 28th Feb the last day of the month we moved at 9 p.m. to a place called Hertogenbosche for a rest. We were billeted in a school after a long journey, so the lads were not long in getting their beds down.

I was detailed next day for the Sgts. Mess as a waiter, so I was excused all duties. It was long hours but I didn't mind that, as it was easy work, also very good food, which was served.

The following nights many flying bombs were going over. A few dropped in our area shaking the place violently, as it was a big building.

We moved again on Tuesday 6th March at 1.30 p.m. for another long journey into Belgium to continue our rest. We were in civvy billets so everyone was satisfied as it was more comfortable than the school. The village was a fair size and was not far from Leopoldburg a large town of many people.

It was on Thursday night the 8th March that I was going for a rest at the "Red Lion Club" the place I had worked at for weeks. I packed my kit ready for the morning and past a peaceful night in bed.

The next morning, I left at 8.30 for this village called Braine L'Alleud, which I arrived at 1.30 p.m. The staff, were very surprised to see me, so I received a hearty welcome from all. I stayed at the Covent till Tuesday morning the 13th, where I left at 9.30 after a very pleasant and well satisfied stay. I went to dances, cinema's and shows, which were very good. I went to Brussels one morning which was 12 miles away by tram to collect my photo's, which I had done in Feb but the fellow had mislaid my address, so I was lucky to be that way at the time.

After my return to harbour the following days were spent on training of all different types for the assault crossing of the Rhine, which was our next big task.

Whenever we crossed canals and rivers a great deal of planning went into it. On a number of occasions I would be part of a reconnaissance party of about six men. We would go out at night down to the river bank in order to work out what equipment and supplies would be needed in order for our troops to cross. Before we set off on these missions we would black up our hands and put on balaclavas so that we could not be seen by the enemy who were often on the opposite river bank. We also had to jump up and down in front of an officer in order for him to know that we had no keys, coins or anything in our pockets that would make a noise when we moved that might be heard by the enemy. On the other hand we often saw German soldiers on the opposite bank lighting up cigarettes in the dark; we obviously couldn't shoot at them because it would give our position away.

On Sat 17th March we were inoculated in each arm with T.A.B. and T.T. so we couldn't do much in the way of work or exercise, as it was very painful and sore.

On Monday 19th our section which was 13 men, including N.C.O's had the advance job of clearing the Companies harbour in Germany near the Rhine. We had a very long journey in front of us, so we prepared for the worst and made sure of a good soft seat. We arrived at our destination at 2.30 p.m. where upon we cooked a light meal from "Compo" packs. After this we were detailed off for different work such as clearing trees, rubble, also filling in craters and bad ruts caused by tanks earlier on in the battle. The weather was really lovely so our task was an easy one. We went shooting with our rifles in the forest, for a bit of so-called practise. This I enjoyed very much, as I am very fond of that type of sport.
The Company came on Wed morning at 4.30 a.m. so much sleep was lost by all, which was made up next day in the sun, a healthy way for a tired person.

It was on Thursday 22nd March that we were all briefed for the crossing of the Rhine, which was to take place on Sat 24th. The weather was lovely and sunny, just the right type for operations. The lads left the harbour at

11.30 p.m. for a 6 mile march carrying all tools and equipment. Myself, I stayed at the harbour as the batman went on leave, so I dropped for his job for a fortnight, which suited me very well at the time.

On Sat 24th a terrific barrage opened up to aid the crossing. After this was followed the Airborne invasion of which was the biggest operation every known. They came over in their thousands. We watched them for 3 hrs going over without a stop. All of us by this time were very keyed up as to see all these planes and gliders gave us great confidence and pride. We saw many planes come back on fire, some of them landed near us, so we ran over to give any assistance but the heat was too much for us. I could see the pilot inside un-strapping himself, the fire was getting worse but he managed to free himself and clambered out. He was not badly hurt, so he was able to ride away to collect his crew who had bailed out earlier on.

This Airborne invasion was known as Operation Varsity and was highly successful, unlike the ill fated Operation Market Garden in September 1944. Our aircraft would tow the gliders, which carried up to 22 men, then release them to land on flat ground. The soldiers would quickly jump out and disappear into nearby woods and surrounding countryside. Of over 400 gliders that landed only 88 remained undamaged by enemy fire or crash landing. Many pilots died but thousands of paratroops were dropped successfully.

We moved at 12.30 after having a rushed dinner. We went to the waiting area ready for crossing. We stayed here until 4.30 p.m. on Sunday 25th where we went across the Rhine on a class 9 raft. The river was about 420 yds wide, so the current was fairly strong. We met the platoon at a badly damaged farm, who were preparing a meal of eggs and chips, as the ration hadn't come across yet.

The small village was called Merhr, where white flags were blowing in the wind. The civilians looked very amazed as to all the transport and men, which were all round about. The following days I managed to do a little washing, also write a few letters, which I was behind with.

We moved again on Good Friday to the place where the paratroopers had landed, so all scattered about were gliders and parachutes, so the lads were out souvenir hunting.

I actually slept in a glider one night which did not impress my Officer who pointed out that it was made of wood and if hit by enemy fire I could have burned to death!

We moved again on Sat 31 March to a new better harbour at Dingden, a small German village, which hadn't seen much shelling. We were in a very good farm, plenty of eggs and chicken.

On Monday 2nd April we were visited by General Barber, our Division Commander, so we had plenty of cleaning to do. He congratulated us all on our splendid courage and cheerfulness in the last operation. He spoke how we cleared mines and kept the roads open for the Div transport, which was very important for the lads up the front.

We moved next day Tuesday 3rd April for a 57 mile ride to a place called Errich. We stayed here just for one night.
We moved next morning at 9.30 through streets laden with civvies pulling carts, all looking very surprised. White flags hung from every house telling us they had enough of the war. We saw many Polish prisoners who had been brought to Mesum to work under German force labour. They spoke how badly the Germans had treated them, for 5 years. Their food was 1 loaf of bread between 5 men a day, which is not very much. They told us how they were made to work on the roads by day and in the factory by night, having very little sleep at all. So they were very pleased to see us and to smoke an English cigarette.

We moved on Friday morning at 7.45 a.m. for a very long journey, which took us 26hrs, so we were all very tired and dirty. The drivers had very little rest, so it was very hard going for them. We saw many German prisoners coming back from the front, looking very tired and weary, as we were not giving them any chance of resting. We arrived at a place called Bingden at 9.30, so the lads were not very long in getting settled down for a few hours well wanted sleep.

On Sunday 8th April we moved again at 7.30 for a bridging job over the river Weser. We went through a village, which hadn't been thoroughly cleared, so everyone was ready for anything, which may have come our way but nothing seriously happened only one sniper had a pop shot at us but he was soon treated by the lads. We slept that night in a farm, which we found out later to belong to the German musician Wagner. A lovely big house of many well furnished rooms, so our short stay was very enjoyable as the lads had plenty of things to look over.

Wagner's house was like a mansion, it was magnificent, and it was obvious that it belonged to a musician because there was a large piano and a lot of things associated with music. There were servants and people who worked in the building living in the basement. I now think that this place may have been Bayreuth Festival Opera House, not far from Osnabruck, which Wagner had built before he died in 1883. I believe it is still used for concerts today. Before we left I took a silver serviette ring and a hand-stitched table cloth as souvenirs. After the war I stupidly sold the serviette ring quite cheaply but I still have the table cloth.

On Monday morning we rose at 5.30 to start bridging, as it was a big job we had on hand. The other Companies helped us, so we were finished at 4.30 in the afternoon after an all out effort, so we moved back to Minden for a wash and some sleep, as I thought but as usual I was on guard. Still I had second shift so things weren't so bad.

On Wednesday 11th April we moved at 7.30 for a long journey of 70 miles, until we made contact with the enemy, which we found to be "SS" troops in a wood east of Thorise. It was this village we slept for the night only to move next afternoon at 3.30 p.m. to a town, which had only just been taken, called Celle. A very nice place to look at but as it was a German place no one took much interest about the place, only to loot as much as possible, which was very enjoyable by all ranks.

We had contact with the 'S.S.' on several occasions. We were quite wary of them because we knew how ruthless they could be, not only when fighting the enemy but in dealing with civilians. They had a reputation for being mad and unpredictable and many of them were believed to be 'high' on drugs of some sort. This seemed to be true because when we found their bodies their skin would be very dark, even black, which was evidently probably due to the drug-taking.

It was on Friday 13th that I moved away from Celle on a truck for leave. We travelled to 624 Field Park where we stayed the night in a civvy house, making ourselves very comfortable with the bedding that was at hand.

We moved away next morning at 9.30 and covered 150 miles in a 3 tonner, so we were very tired and dusty, as the roads were bad for quick travelling. We stopped at a town for the night, which had been a public house but as they couldn't get any beer there was plenty of room for all of us.

On Sunday 15th we arrived at Genappe transit camp, where we waited all day without any luck of getting on the train. We watched a game of football, then retired to our tent for a good nights sleep, which we all needed.

We were up early next morning to see if we could get away that day, so we hung about the tents listening to the band also the loudspeaker, which didn't call on us until 4.30 p.m. so we rushed forward obtained a ticket and then packed up ready for the train, which was due to leave at 5.30 so we didn't bother about any tea. The train left that evening at 7 p.m. for a 12hr journey for Calais. We travelled all night snatching odd spots of sleep where we could, as the seats were very uncomfortable.

We arrived next morning Monday 16th April at 7.30, so we didn't loose anytime in getting a wash, as we felt very dirty, then to breakfast, which I needed badly. We sailed at 1.30 p.m. from Calais on a well-laden boat of happy faces all bound for Blighty. We got half way across the Channel and then it was we saw the glorious sight of the White Cliffs of Dover. We arrived in port at 3.30 but never got off until 4 o'clock, as there were so many going to the London area, of which I was one of them. Arrived home 9.30 Tues April 17th.

The following days were lovely and fine, so we travelled about to Littlehampton, London and the surrounding districts, which were all very enjoyable.

Sunday 22nd April, which was girlfriends birthday, so we all had a big party of 16 to tea so it made a lot of work for Mother. It was lovely to see all the relations at home at the same time as I had done enough travelling about getting here, so that was the best way I spent Sunday, talking and laughing of the things of the past, which amused everyone present.

It was obviously great to go on leave after being away from home for so long and everyone was so pleased to see me. I spent as much time as possible with my family and girl friend and also went out for a few, well quite a few, beers with my mates! Some of them were away fighting for the Country but those at home all wanted to know what I had been up to in the fight against Adolph. I did tell them a bit when asked but I found it difficult, partly because unless you have actually experienced the horrors, excitement and dangers of war it is impossible to fully understand what it's like and secondly I couldn't forget my mates still out there fighting and I was soon to rejoin them. It's not the fault of the folks at home; it's just like living in two different worlds.

Monday 23rd April was a glorious sunny morning, so I took girlfriend to town to have a look round the shops, as I needed a few oddments.

1945 the lads relaxing – Gerry is holding the football.

The lads at occupied house in Germany which they used as a billet for several days.

Gerry, on right, and friend.
The Regimental sign was made by Gerry.

Gertrude in German uniform. She was thought to be a member of the SS, absconded and worked on a farm with Margarete. She remained good friends with Gerry and Margarete for many years.

Gerry befriending local German children.

Gerry, on left, and pals. Lauenberg Germany 1946.

Gerry, second right, and pals at a billet in 1946.

Gerry, extreme right, at Lauenburg Bridge.

Lauenburg Bridge, re-constructed 1946. Many bridges were blown up by the Germans in 1945 in order to slow down the advancing allies.

Bridge building - the final stages.

Sign commemorating the re-building of Artlenburg Bridge.

Artlenburg Bridge re-built by the Royal Engineers 1946.

Gerry, on right, and friends take a break from bridgebuilding.

Royal Engineers, 15th Scottish Regiment, Detmold Barracks, 1947. Gerry is extreme left 2nd row from top.

Gerry and Margarete on
their wedding day.

They were married on 9th January 1948 at Detmold, Germany.

Gerry and Margarete spent a few days of their honeymoon in Berlin where they saw the result of allied bombing. This is the Potsdamer Platz before the war.

and at the end of the war.

Ruins of the German Chancellery.

The Chancellery – the Diplomats Room in ruins.

Der Kaiserhof- Hitler's Hotel.

Hitler's Bunker.

GERMANY

On Tuesday 24th April was my last full day of leave, so I was out making the most of it. I went to the pictures where a good enjoyable film was being shown.

Next day I was up early as I had a lot of visiting to do, so I mended my puncher in my cycle and set off for my relations in town. I arrived back for dinner at 12.30, which I thoroughly enjoyed, as the fresh air of early morning had given me an appetite.

I was to catch the train that evening at 7.15 p.m. so it meant leaving home at 6.45. I said goodbye to my father, who owing to illness was confined to his bed so Mother came with me to the station, also girlfriend and sister and her father who had come home for the evening. The parting on the station was not so bad as I had expected, so I left without a tear being shed on either side, which was very satisfying.

I journeyed to Victoria with a friend from my own town, so I was very glad of the company. We arrived at Victoria at 9.30 so we visited the Y.M.C.A. for a small snack before leaving at 10.30 on the Dover troop train, which was well laden with troops from a great variety of divisions. We arrived at Dover at 1.30, where we were taken in lorries to a big barracks where we stayed until the following morning Thursday 26th then we went for the boat, which was to take us across the channel to Calais.

We arrived at Calais at 10 o'clock. After having breakfast, I sat down to write a few urgent letters. We caught the train from Calais at 3.30 p.m. for a journey of 12hrs to the transit camp at Genappe, where upon we arrived at 4.30 a.m. of Friday 27th April, so we had breakfast then retired to some well desired sleep.

On Sat 28th we moved to the new leave camp at Osnabruck, a lovely city that had been badly hit by our bombers in recent raids. After travelling the following days to different camps, I arrived back at the company who were over the river Elbe at a farm. That night we were called out for a bridging job. At 2 o'clock in the morning we set off feeling very tired and annoyed. We arrived back from our task at 7.30, so the first thing we required was our bed, so very few went for breakfast.

The next morning Wed 2nd May we were up early for a move to a village called Brunsdorf, where we only stayed for a few hours for food. The next village where we stayed the night was where we were shelled for the last time, it was here that we heard about Hitler and Goebels committing suicide, so everyone were much more cheerful than before. We moved into another village called Trittau where we stayed for 2 or 3 days, so we were able to write a few letters, of which we were very behind with owing to all these moves. We saw hundreds upon hundreds of Jerry soldiers flocking past without escort, some travelling and driving their own lorries, which were heavily laden.

An incident happened about this time and near the end of the war which had a lasting effect on me and it still upsets me even today when I think about it. We were advancing through Germany and were somewhere in the Black Forrest, I can't remember exactly where, because I couldn't write about it in my Diary at the time.

 We were being shelled by the enemy who were hidden in bunkers under thick trees. Our aircraft tried bombing them but without much success as the bombs were exploding when they hit the trees. I was up in our front line when suddenly two Germans, one an Officer, appeared through the trees waving a white flag. The Officer spoke perfect English and said that he had about six hundred men in his bunkers and he wanted to surrender. We radioed back to get an escort to take the two Germans to our HQ. While we were waiting I commented to the Officer that he spoke very good English and he said that he had gone to school in England. He asked if any of us came from Worthing! On telling him that I did he asked me if I knew of Lancing College (which is a Public School near Worthing) and he told me he was a pupil there before the war. Talk about 'a small world'! The Officer and his colleague were then taken to negotiate his surrender and after a while returned to their men. I don't know the reason but their surrender was not accepted. A short time later a number of our armoured vehicles advanced to our position and then into the forest towards the enemy. The vehicles were flame-throwers that spewed out nitro-glycerine which sucks out all oxygen from enclosed spaces. All the German bunkers, which were mainly made of wood with straw as a floor covering, were obliterated. Many of the enemy soldiers came out of the bunkers head to toe in flames and were burnt to death or shot. All six hundred were killed within three hours, including the ex-Lancing college schoolboy. For obvious reasons I did not write about this in my Diary and unsurprisingly there is no account of it in the Official Records. War is so cruel. Today, when I see Lancing College, I am sadly reminded of that German Officer

On Monday 7th May we moved at 9 o'clock for Kiel, where we arrived at 6.30. We saw the damage done by our bombers, which was opening to the average eye.

It was on Tuesday 8th May that we heard the great outstanding news about the resistance in Europe had ceased, so everyone was very happy, so songs were the only way of celebrating.

This was VE (Victory in Europe Day) the end of the war! I can't remember exactly what my feelings were except that we were all so relieved and happy and celebrated by singing, drinking, getting drunk and generally going a bit mad! Although the fighting had finished we knew we still had a lot to do and would not be going back to England for a while.

Next day Wed 9th May we had a party for the whole platoon, including wines, beer and spirits, so everyone including the officer were very merry and singing at the tops of their voices.

On Thursday morning we went out in a lorry to view Kiel, as it is such a large port. We went over the very large road bridge, which was many feet from the ground, as people walking below looked like toys. The docks were littered with sunken vessels of all types, including his famous sea weapon the "U" boat. They lay there damaged or scuttled by their crews so as they couldn't be any use to us.

On Friday 11th May it was very sunny and hot, so watching a football match was the ideal thing for us but for the players it was very exhausting. Still it was a good game, where we lost four three. The civilians were made to clear all the rubbish from the streets by the military, so we watched from our billet windows, a sight I will never forget. The same day my pal from the Div club arrived with fresh news of the Division, which we hadn't heard of.

On Monday 14th I was on guard all night and to my surprise when being posted sentry, I had a Jerry as a mate, a very unusual thing and to think I had been fighting them a few days previous. Still he was harmless as he did not carry arms but me not taking any chances I had one round up the breech just in case I said a word out of place.

Wednesday 16th May the whole platoon went for the day to Plon about 12 miles away, where we enjoyed ourselves rowing or swimming. My opinion of the water after I had got up to my knees was much to cold, so I didn't venture any further. It was a beautiful day so rowing on this large lake was very enjoyable by all. We returned in the evening with a large appetite, which was soon put right by the cooks who had a hot dinner waiting for us.

On Friday 18th May we saw on orders the men which this Division had lost since Normandy, they are as follows:- Wounded were 669 officers with 11,422 other ranks. Those killed were 181 officers and 2,793 other ranks. So reading these orders brought back memories of which one tries to forget.

When I started writing my Diary after landing in Normandy I kept a list of all the lads in our Unit and Platoon who were killed or injured. After a few weeks I stopped because there were so many. From my Unit of the original 150 who were there when I joined in 1944 only 20 of us survived.

(It is interesting that The Official War Records of 278 Company only record the deaths of certain Senior Officers. There is a column headed 'Other Ranks Where Return To The Unit Is Particularly Required.' This records the names of various junior ranks who were missing from their Unit and amongst the reasons given were 'Believed prisoner of war' 'Injured, in hospital in UK' 'Whereabouts not known.' Some names appear on this list for many months and one can only assume that some of them might have unfortunately been killed, although that fact is not recorded in the Official War Records which are now held at the Public Records Office; one presumes the details were recorded in Regimental Records).

Also censorship has ceased, so we were able to write letters at ease without giving a thought who was to have read them, only the person which was to receive it. We were called upon for a job which was guarding the vaults of the Reichbank, Kiel, which had been bombed. So 8 of us were picked, as gold coins had been located. So we had strict orders for anyone who made a false move, they took out that day 600,000 gold sovereigns, so Germany had been hoarding British currency of which the value was double now. Also, gold bars, all came to England.

I only wrote brief details at the time about this incident at the Bank because we were told not to talk to anyone about it. I and a few other lads were specially selected for this task under the supervision of an Officer. The building had been badly damaged by our bombs and it was pretty well flattened with most of the basement, where the vaults were, under water. Each of us had two Germans each to look after who did the digging which took about three days. On reaching the vaults we placed three explosives and blew the safes open. It was quite a dangerous exercise because we were in a confined area. They contained not only the gold sovereigns but a large number of gold bars. I never did really find out where this valuable haul had come from but I think it was from dealings that the German Bank had with the Bank of England before the war. We were instructed to load the gold bars, which were in boxes and very heavy, onto a lorry and we took them to the docks where they were loaded onto a British ship. The whole operation was overseen by two men, both English and not in uniform, who we believed were from the Bank of England. They said absolutely nothing and even the briefcases they carried had black tape covering their initials. Every move we made was closely watched, from the Bank until the boxes containing the gold bars were safely on the ship ready to be taken back to England. When we finished the job we were searched and again told not to tell anyone about what we had done and I never spoke about it to my mates or family.

(Research shows that between 1945 and 1947 approx. £1.5bn in gold, cash, art collections and jewellery disappeared from various Reichbank across Germany. Much of this was the vast spoils of war that the Nazi leaders had attempted to hide but the Americans are believed to have recovered about £300 million hidden in a remote salt mine. However, it is thought that of the £3.2bn the Nazis had amassed about half remains unaccounted for. It may have been taken by Allied governments as part of a plan to rebuild their economies or perhaps some by opportunistic liberating soldiers, we will never know. Gerry's account of being ordered to remove gold bars and sovereigns from the bank in Kiel under strict secrecy certainly raises questions and seems to give some credence to the mystery. Nothing is recorded in Official Regimental Records

The following days the Platoon played cricket, also attended regular picture shows where good films were being seen, so the morale was a little brighter. Our officer Lt. Whalley, started schools in the afternoons, so many lads attended to the subject of mathematics at its early stages and then as the days went on he increased the lessons. So evenings and spare periods you could see fellows puzzling their brains over difficult figures using plenty of paper in the course of an hour.

On Friday 25th May was fine and sunny, so our cruise around the harbour of Kiel was very pleasant, as it was a great change. Also, we saw all the war weapons of Jerry, such as his "U" boats by the score. Some damaged, scuttled and some intact. We saw one Jerry battleship, which had been crippled by our bombers and left in dry dock un-repairable.

Sunday May 27th was my 20th birthday, which I spent travelling to our Field Park Company to work at my trade, so as I could pick up knowledge, which I had forgotten in the past. The following days I spent in the workshop very interested in what I was doing, as I was eager to get on. We had some very bad thunderstorms, mostly evenings, so plenty of letters were written as one couldn't go out in such weather.

Wed June 6th was a day off as it was the anniversary of "D" day. To think the Armies of the Allies had cleared the continent in 1 year, a great achievement by all arms.

On Wed 13th June, we moved at 8.30 for a long journey to a place called Schwerin, a town near a large lake where the Russians were the other side, so we occasionally came across them evenings while out for a walk. We were in a Jerry barracks on the edge of this lake so the appearance of the place was great, as it was neatly laid out to plan.   I sat the first night writing letters and in between I gazed through the window on a statue of a youth who caught every passer by. As one thinks of the fanatical youth, which had in the past, pride, strength and vigour but owing to one man, a dictator all was lost in a cruel war of which they lost after heavy losses were inflicted.

On Sat 16th June we attended a large parade, which included all the infantry of our brigade, as the Army commander was to talk to us on our fight and struggles since "D" day.   The pipe band was there, all dressed in their colours and in perfect timing.   The following days I spent working on the wood machines in the shop with great interest. In the evenings I went with my mate on the large lake where we could use motor launches at ease for an hour or so, which was very enjoyable as the weather was sunny and warm making perfect evenings but like all good things they must come to an end.

So on the 30th June we moved back to Bad Segeberg, were we were before for a few weeks.   We arrived safely into some houses, which were of a low state for living in.   So the next day we were cleaning the place up making it look a bit decent.   We were all very unsettled, as the place seemed dead after our times at Schwerin, a lovely city. My first job was to help build a new guardroom, so I was employed for many days, which we hung out as long as possible.

On Friday 13th we had a party as one fellow was leaving us for civvy street.   The drink was plentiful, so of course we drunk with ease but myself being a light drinker, I was over-come and staggered over to my billets after being sick at the Guardroom.   I layed on my bed with my head going round and round.   I managed to fall asleep but next morning I was not fit to go on parade, so I took over billet orderly.   Over the weekend I recovered after going to the lake sunbathing and rowing, which I think, done me good.

The following weeks I attended the lake regular, as the café there called Ilsee served English beer, so we spent many a good evening there.   I visited a farm house which my friend was not very keen on, as he was more interested in going with the German girls, as now the ban was lifted so it made things easier for some of the lads.   The occupants were 3 Belgians and 2 Frenchmen of the Military Government, who were waited upon by the women and two daughters of the house.   So we held many a evening there *drinking port wine of good quality. They were able to speak English, so it was not difficult to make conversation at any time.*

On Tuesday 14th August the Japanese war finished so our infantry put up a grand show of fireworks and flares, which made me think of the war and my pals who gave their lives for a cause, which they will not benefit on this earth.

On Wednesday 5th Sept I left Bad Segeberg much to my regret, as I was well and truly settled for entertainment and work. The company was at Reinbek, a small town 18 miles from Hamburg, so again I had to settle down as everything had changed to when I had left them 3 months ago.

The day arrived when I was to go on leave, which was Monday 10th Sept at 9.30 a.m. We rode to Hamburg's transit camp where we stayed till 4.30 p.m. Then we boarded the train for our long journey to Rotterdam, where we had a wash and shave, which we needed badly as the journey was a rough one.

We left that night Tuesday 11th Sept at 9 p.m. on a large troop ship all fitted out for the purpose. The trip over, took 9 hrs of which I slept five hours, as it was calm but very warm as there were so many troops on boards. I arrived home at 1 p.m. just in time for dinner but it was a long dinner as I had so much to talk about. I made good use of my days by helping Father make a new coke box, which Mother was in great need of. I also took girlfriend to London where we spent all day looking round different places of interest. We saw in Trafalgar Square the famous inventions of Germany, the "V" weapons, the most outstanding the V.2. as it stood on end as though it was ready for firing. It attracted many people as it mystified many in the past. After a very pleasant leave I returned to my unit after a very rough passage, which made many lads sick. The unit had build a lovely club with a stage combined and had called it the "Forty Niners", which was our unit number. The lighting was run off a generator in the camp, so lights were numerous and in different colours. I spent many a good evening at the club as we had shows every night and dances twice a week. Beer was served every night if available, but tea and cakes were always on sale along with the wines and lemonades. The club had obtained from Radio Hamburg a lovely musician, who we called Albert but he was always announced as The King of the Accordion, as he knew so beautifully every note and tune, which we listened too with great attention, as his music sweet and pleasant soothed and cheered ones thoughts.

Then a sad day came when I had to leave the unit on a posting to the 7th Armoured Division or the "Desert Rats". I went with one or two of my pals but we arrived at a very lonely spot 5 miles from the nearest town called Itzehoe. I stayed in many nights, as it was cold outside and being a new place I was lost and unhappy, as it were.

Many months past after many enjoyable evenings, either at shows, pictures, walks or the usual, of kicking a ball about while the light lasted.   The weather looked as though summer had really come as it was warm but as it is so changeable over here we did not rely on it, which was very wise as it changed to cold winds and rain just like winter again.   So we sat once again around the fires chatting of many subjects, the chief one of course was demob.

I was kept busy many evenings attending to the lads who came to me for medical treatment, as I had all the first aid equipment required.
I did not mind these sort of evenings as I had interest in this kind of work and the lads appreciated all what I done for them.
One Wednesday afternoon our troop was playing football against H.Q. it was a fast game as the bets were large, such as 3,000 marks (£75) and two bottles of Whisky. Our troop being the best team, they won four to one. They were very exhausted, also many had cuts and bruises, which made walking difficult as the knees suffered the most owing to the hard ground, which had been dried by the sun of the past days.

The town where we were stationed, was called Lochstedger Lager, where the Germans made torpedoes in the underground factories and were moved by train at night times. The ordinance companies were moving shells, etc from the other bunkers to destroy them by burning, which was done day and night for months.

When the war finished in May 1945 218 Field Company was kept very busy in what was called 'works services.' This included repairing roads and bridges, restoring water and electricity supplies and generally helping the local population to recover from the devastation that their retreating army had caused and from allied bombing. We were also responsible for the evacuation and repatriation of some Displaced Persons and Prisoners of War. As a result of all this we were constantly on the move from one town or village to another depending on where we were needed.

Eventually 278 Company was disbanded on 30th April 1946 and I was posted to 211 Field Company where the work carried on as before. The Official Record reported that there was a lot of pressure to carry out the works services. At first there was no proper accommodation for the troops and we were billeted in scattered villas and farmhouses. There was an acute shortage of officers and supervision was almost impossible. Also there was a shortage of tradesmen and stores. There were problems with some of the Military Governments that were set up to deal with the various contracts with German firms and also any complaints from civilians. The problem was the Garrison Commander, head of the local Military Government, had absolutely no powers and had to refer complaints to the German Regional Military Government. This all took time so in general there was sometimes a great deal of confusion. We had to carry on with our duties as best we could.

Our next move was to Detmold into a German barracks, which was very well built. I think the date was around October or November 1946. We quickly settled in here as we were given sheets for the first time and getting regular meals in a good cookhouse. I travelled around the area as I could speak German, buying up timber for our company to make sign boards for the other companies requirements.

It was here that the German girl I got very friendly with at Bad Segeberg came to Detmold to be with me. We found a room for her to stay in, as she had no papers. So I had to give the owners of the house, coffee and cigarettes so as she would not be found out. We enjoyed each other's company for many months, keeping inside the law as we could. We found we loved one another very much, so we decided we would get married but the long wait of months was very trying but we had to fill in a lot of forms and get permission from the Army. Which we did and we were married in the Army Church in Detmold on 9th Jan 1948. We only had friends at our wedding, as no relations could come. The following day the police arrived to arrest my wife, as they had found out she was staying in the area without papers but of course they could not do anything now, as she had become a

British Army wife. They looked at the papers and left.
I was demobbed in March of this year and we both came to England to meet all my relations and friends, which was difficult for her, as she couldn't speak any English.

Lancing College near Worthing where the German Officer who wanted to surrender attended prior to the war.

Gerry and Margarete – Golden wedding anniversary January 1998.

Margarete's grave in Worthing.

August 2011 – Gerry remembers his beloved wife, Margarete.

Gerry's war medals. Left to right ; 1939 – 1945 Star. France/
Germany Star. The British Defence medal (given to Gerry for
his service in the Home Guard) and 1939 – 1945
British war medal.

Gerry with his diary.

MARGARETE

Sunday 3rd June 1945 was a day that would change my life forever. We were in Bad Segeberg billeted in private homes, eight or ten to a house, with a lance-corporal named Jacky in charge.

On that day he told me he had seen two pretty German girls, one blonde and one brunette, that we should go and see them and that I could go with the blonde and he would go with the brunette. We found the girls walking up the road and followed them. At that time, although the war had finished, we were forbidden to talk to any Germans and when they went into a small cafe we sat at another table near them. I spoke fairly good German by then and quietly asked the waiter to serve the girls with beers which I paid for.

When the girls left we followed them to a farm where they were living. We spoke to them and they told us that they were staying at the farm because they had no official papers and couldn't work so were helping out with the milking and cleaning and were sleeping in a cow shed. They told us that they came from different parts of Germany and had met at the farm. They had left their homes because the Russians were in control and they were treating the people very badly. Many young girls were being raped and so they had decided to travel to an area where they would feel safer. I felt sorry for them, returned to my billet where I picked up some coffee, chocolate and cigarettes and went back to the farm. The blonde was named Margarete and the brunette Gertrude. They were delighted to have met us and after having a cup of coffee with them Jacky and I arranged to see them again. I was immediately attracted to Margarete. I knew from that moment it was not a good idea to write about Margarete in my Diary, a wise decision, as a relationship between an English soldier and a German girl was not the kind of thing I thought either the German or my British Superiors would like.

Over the next few weeks Jacky and I saw quite a bit of the girls but had to be very careful because of the ban on British troops fraternising with the Germans. One place we thought was safe was near a place called Lake Ilsee. One day we were all relaxing in a cornfield near the lake, Jacky and I had our jackets undone and our belts off, then suddenly we were discovered by a Major and Sergeant! We were told to get dressed properly and were a disgrace to the Army. We both saluted and were ordered back to our billet. We heard nothing more about the incident but a few days later the ban on talking to the Germans was lifted which was great news. As a result Jacky and I saw a lot of Gertrude and Margarete over the next few weeks. One day we were out walking with them when the Major passed us. He had a big grin on his face and winked at us – we gave him a faultless salute!

At that time Margarete could speak little English but I could speak some German and was learning the language fast. One day we went for a drink at the Lake Ilsee cafe and there was a Sergeant sitting with us at the table. When I went to the toilet Margarete dropped her ring in my beer and when I returned he told me what she had done. He told us both that what she had done was a good luck sign and informed Margarete that she would marry me one day! I drank my beer being careful not to swallow the ring and gave it back to her. I had tears in my eyes thinking what a wonderful gesture. Margarete and I were getting very fond of each other; in fact we were falling in love. We often spent night's together and made love. Of course I was engaged to a girl back home but I realised that I would have to face some big decisions.

One day I was with Margarete at the farm and it was a very hot day. I had noticed that Gertrude always had a plaster on her left shoulder and, possibly because of the sweat, it fell off. I noticed that she had a number and three dots in the shape of a triangle tattooed on her shoulder. I knew that this meant she had been in some way connected to the S.S. Gertrude told us that the main reason she had run away was because of the terrible way she had been treated. Evidently throughout the war the German officers would use large lorries, fitted out with bunk beds, in which they would keep six to eight girls for them to have sex with and she had been one of them. Sometime later in the war we captured similar lorries with girls still in them, also refrigerated vehicles loaded with vegetables which we gladly sent back to our cooks. I said nothing to anyone about Gertrude as I didn't want to get involved and thought that if the authorities found out it may affect my relationship with Margarete. However, a French Officer who was staying at the farm and I think having a relationship with the daughter of the woman who owned it had also noticed Gertrude's tattoo and reported it. She was arrested and I later heard sent to prison for two years for being absent without leave and having no papers. Because of what had happened to Gertrude Jacky was upset and never went back to the farm. It was probably a good thing as I later found out that he was married back in England! After the war had ended Gertrude came to Detmold where Margarete and I were living. She was very grateful for the kindness I had shown when she was at the farm but she also thought we might have reported her. We told her it was the French Officer which she was relieved to hear and we remained good friends.

I will never forget Gertrude for one very good reason. When I found out about her possible connection to the S.S. I wanted to write about it in my diary but I knew if I did and it was ever read by the British or Germans I would be in terrible trouble. At the time I was a young lad and, like many of my mates, experimenting with 'do-it-yourself tattoos'. Anyway, so that I would remember Gertrude's story to write about later, at least that's why I think I did it, I tattooed the sign of the S.S., three dots, on my arm. A bit stupid I suppose, in fact very bloody stupid, and heaven knows what the Germans would have made of it if I had been captured! I still have the tattoo to this day.
By now Margarete and I had become very close, declaring our love for each other, but our idyllic time together was about to come to an end. We were to move but didn't know exactly where at the time so I wasn't able to tell Margarete that I was going to a place called Reinbek. We had a very tearful parting. Soon after arriving in Reinbek I went on a short leave back to England.

Meanwhile, after I had left her in Bad Segeberg, Margarete had been told by an interpreter where I had gone and ten days later she left the farm and made her way to Reinbek via Hamburg, about eighty miles. She had no papers and little money and travelled mainly at night and on the outside of trains, that's how much she loved me. She told me that many people who had no money would travel on the outside of trains and she even saw some fall off and killed. Margarete had remembered that all the lorries in our unit had the number 42 in white letters on a blue square painted on the side and on reaching Reinbek station she made enquiries and found out where we were. She approached the Sentry on Guard Duty and asked for Gerry Tiller. After a few minutes she was met by a Sapper Tiller, Bill Tiller, no relation, who told her I was on leave in England and due back soon.

Margerete was devastated and returned to the station. It was getting dark and she knew that if she was on the streets after 11 pm she would be arrested. A kind local man on a bike, on seeing her distress and hearing her story offered to take her to his house to share a room with his partner. She accepted the offer and stayed with the couple for a few days sleeping on the floor.

While I was on leave in Worthing I had had a lovely time with my parents, friends and girlfriend, Thelma, to whom I was still engaged. But I couldn't stop thinking about Margerete. I felt really bad about not being fair to Thelma, but at that stage I didn't know if I would ever see Margerete again, I did not know she was waiting for me back in Reinbek and I had no idea what the future was going to be.

When I returned from leave I was told about Margarete looking for me and I knew I had to find her. The local postman informed me that he knew a blonde girl with a rucksack had been seen with a man with a bike at the station a few days earlier and he thought she was at his house. I found the place and we were both 'over the moon' at seeing each other again. I think at that moment we realised that it was our destiny to be together for the rest of our lives. I paid the man with the bike handsomely with cigarettes and coffee for what he had done for Margarete, also the postman who offered Margarete a room in his house with his wife which she happily accepted.

We were worried because Margarete had no money or papers but the postman managed to get her a job as a cook in the soup kitchen in Reinbek. Her job was to make vegetable soup in a huge copper vat for the poor people of the town. She found it very hard work but it was satisfying because she got paid and was given her work permit. She was happy living with the postman and his wife in the village called Shoningshadt and we all became very good friends. One day Margarete told me that the postman was hardly able to walk as he had a badly infected foot. There were very few doctors about at that time and knowing that I had first aid experience in the Army she asked me to have a look at it. I agreed and using brandy and salt water as an antiseptic I managed to lance the poor postman's infected toe with my scalpel. He was so grateful to be free of pain and after about a week he was able to go back to work.

During this time I had my normal Army duties such as Guard Duty but Margarete and I managed to see each other quite often. We always knew that I would have to leave her at any time because Germany was in a terrible mess. Their Army had retreated and surrendered and Montgomery wanted our troops to push on and, together with the Americans, take control of Berlin for political reasons; unfortunately the Russians got there first which was to change the history of the Country for many years to come.

After several weeks Margarete had a few days holiday from her job and decided to go back to her home village called Bad Wilsnack and see her parents who did not know where she was or even if she was still alive. I was very worried as we knew that the Russians were in control of all the checkpoints she would have to go through to get home and I had heard stories about the dreadful way the Russians treated the civilian population, particularly young girls. We asked several people who had travelled similar journeys and they told Margarete the best route to take. I gave her a few bottles of vodka, lots of coffee and cigarettes which she used to bribe the Russians at crossing points. Our parting was so sad, she could not write or phone or let me know anything and we didn't know if we would ever see each other again. We swore our love for one another and vowed to meet up again someday.

Margarete returned about a week later, much to my surprise, and I was so relieved to see her. She was very tired and wet because she had crossed streams and walked across rough country areas to avoid Russian checkpoints as much as possible. It was difficult for German civilians to move around the Country without the proper papers at that time, which Margarete didn't have. She was still able to stay at the postman's house and he and his wife were so kind to her.
It was obvious that Margarete and I were very devoted to each other.

We made love which was so sincere; we had tears in our eyes but were happy that we were together again. The feelings we had for each other cannot be put into words. I think that at that time we both knew we would get married. I can't really explain it, but from the first day we met when Margarete put her ring in my beer, which at the time I treated as a joke, the more we saw of each other the more the love between us grew. Although the war in Europe was over of course we had no idea what was going to happen to Germany or the population and after the fighting had finished restrictions stayed in place for quite some time. Margarete and I did sometimes talk about getting married but I can't remember that I actually asked her, or got down on my knees or anything like that. The more we fell in love with each other the more it became obvious that we would eventually get married.

Margarete was still able to keep her job at the soup kitchen making soup every day for the poor and homeless people from the area. It was hard work but she found it very satisfying to help the ever growing numbers of suffering people. Also it provided her with a work permit and a little money. We spent many happy hours together going for walks in the evenings when the weather permitted. Then, very sadly, I was told the Unit was moving on again to a place I think was called Lochstedger Leger. It had been a German Army Depot for making arms and torpedos which were made in factories, some underground, and then transported by special trains to the German Navy. While I was there I visited the area underground where the weapons were made, many of them by women and prisoners, and the conditions were very harsh.

Although the war had finished, because the village was about eighty miles from Reinbek it was very difficult for me to travel back to see Margarete and for her to come to see me was out of the question. I had to get a weekend pass which only officially allowed me to travel ten miles from the billet, however, I would leave after lunch on a Friday and the journey took up to four hours. I went by train and 'hitch hiked' and sometimes had to walk about ten miles in all sorts of weather. I went via Hamburg then on to Reinbek and arrived tired, but it was all worth it to see Margarete. My feet were usually sore from wearing boots which wore holes in my socks, which Margarete would sew up for me. We would spend the weekend together, often going to the Cafe for music and dancing. I had to leave Margarete at about six o'clock to get a train to Hamburg. Then, sometimes if I was lucky, I would manage to find an Army vehicle that was going my way and get a lift as far as possible, hopefully near to my billet. I had to be very careful though, because I knew that if I was picked up by the Military Police I would be in trouble for abusing my weekend pass and they would be stopped. Also it was risky, I was supposed to be back by midnight but often didn't get there until 12.30am or 1.00am. The things we do for love!

In October or November 1946 we heard that we were to move again, this time to a large German Barracks at Detmold. I was kept very busy making duckboards, notice boards etc. for the Military Police. We employed twelve German tradesmen every day, painters, plumbers, carpenters and sign writers. I was a Lance Corporal and had many duties to perform including Guard Commander which was a twenty four hour a day responsibility. I was also responsible for the fitness of about fifty soldiers. Every morning, before breakfast, I would take them on a run or march around the streets of Detmold.

Sometimes I would go with Major Duffy to visit German firms who supplied us with wood and paint. I spoke quite good German and so it saved the cost of employing a translator. I would wait for the Major in a side room at the Officers' Mess and he would send the barman out with a lager and a whisky for me which was very welcome!

During this time I was not able to visit Margarete in Reinbek as it was just too far. My letters to her had to be translated into German, and then posted to the postman's house where she was still living. She could not reply to me though as it was not allowed. Also we could not use the telephones, so it was worrying for me not knowing how she was getting on.

Then, one day right out of the blue, the Sentry on Guard Duty sent me a note telling me that a blonde female was at the Sentry box. I immediately rushed to the gate and standing there was my beloved Margarete! She had a rucksack on her back and looked very tired and hungry. I was so happy to see her but upset when she told me she had travelled all the way from Reinbek, mostly on the outside of trains because she didn't have money for the fare.

I went straight away to see a German I knew called Herman and asked him if he could get Margarete a room near the Barracks, because I knew if she stayed out on the streets she would be arrested. Herman arranged for Margarete to stay with a Mr and Mrs Heidaman who had two young boys. I paid them for the room with marks, cigarettes and coffee for which they were very grateful. I then used to buy sandwiches, cakes and other food from the NAFFI and smuggle them out to give to Margarete, which was forbidden. I used to put them inside my tunic and I remember a few times I bought some hard-boiled eggs and put them under my hat! I would meet Margarete on a bench in the park and give her the food for which she was so grateful as she had little money. I remember the very cold winter of 1947 when I gave Margarete my Army greatcoat to put over herself at night to keep warm.

At that time it was not possible to go out with Margarete during the day, we just didn't think it was safe to do so. She had no travel permit and no reason to be in Detmold. If she was found she would have been arrested, we had to be very careful who we spoke to and trusted. My mates were very good though; most of them knew about my German girlfriend and helped us as much as they could.

It was about this time that Major Duffy called me to his office and asked me if I would like to sign on in the Army for another nine years. He told me that if I did I would be promoted to full Corporal in a month and Sergeant in three months. He told me that everyone agreed I was good at my job and well liked. The offer was very tempting but my thoughts at the time were about Margarete and me and our future. I had to turn the offer down which disappointed the Major.

By the summer of 1947 Margarete and I had decided that we should definitely get married. I went on a short leave back to England and broke the news to Thelma that our engagement was off. She was obviously very upset and gave me back the ring. Her father was not at all pleased and told me what he thought of me. He even said I might be taken to Court for 'Breach of Promise' which was an offence in those days! Luckily nothing came of that. My parents were not too pleased either and I remember my sister-in-law saying "Why do you have to go and marry a bloody German?"

Meanwhile, Margarete had to go back to her parents, ask them for permission to marry me and get the various papers signed which were required. She told me that when she informed her father that she wanted to marry an Englishman his remark was- roughly translated into English- "I hope you know what you're doing, don't take him too seriously, he will shit on you!" Sometime later, when I went and met him we got on very well, he, Margaret's Mother and all her family could not have been nicer towards me. In fact, I reminded him of the remarks he had made about me to his daughter and we laughed about it over a few beers!

Margarete and I eventually got married on 9th January 1948 at the Garrison Army Church in Detmold. None of our relatives were there but we received a lot of telegrams and it was the happiest day of my life! We were not allowed to live together though. Margarete was still living with the Heideman family and I had to stay in the Barracks. I was allowed to go and see her every night when I wasn't on duty but had to be back by midnight. The Army did provide us with some food rations every week that we were entitled to as a married couple and which helped out greatly.

We were married on a Friday and on the Saturday morning two plain-clothed German policeman called at the Heideman's house and asked to see Margarete. They said they had been given information that a German girl was staying there illegally and that she had no work permit or papers. Margarete was delighted to show them her marriage certificate and explain that she was married to an English soldier! They apologised and went away.

We decided to go to Berlin for our honeymoon. We thought it was a safe place to go because it was a big city and was being run by the Russians and Americans. The train to Berlin was run by the Russians and all passengers were locked in the carriages, however, when we arrived in the American Sector we felt safe and relaxed. The Army had arranged for us to stay in a hotel which was a disaster and we only stayed there for one night. Our room and bed was full of fleas and Margarete got badly bitten! I was going to complain but she persuaded me not too. We spent the rest of our honeymoon with relatives of Margarete who had a small flat in Berlin and, although we had to sleep on the floor, they and some of their friends made us very welcome.

I was demobbed in March 1948 and returned to England but, because of all the 'red tape' it took several months to get all the official papers and documents that were needed for Margarete to come and settle with me in Worthing.

Eventually the day came when I went up to Victoria Station to meet her. I will never forget seeing her walking along the platform to meet me. We held each other so tightly and, after all we had been through, didn't want to let go. Our lives together were about to start and we were never to be parted again until my darling Margarete sadly died of cancer on 1st January 2005 after over fifty years of very happy marriage.

Of course I do miss her terribly but often visit her grave where she was laid to rest in a beautiful spot in Worthing overlooking the South Downs. I have so much to thank Margarete for, especially all the wonderful happy times we shared together. Between us we proved that 'love will always find a way.'

ON REFLECTION

I do not believe it would be possible for anyone to witness the trauma of war, either as a combatant or as a civilian, without being affected by the experience in some way or other; I am no different. War is a terrible thing and wars today are very different from the one I took part in.

In modern warfare we are quite rightly upset and appalled when we hear of so-called 'collateral damage' which results in the deaths of civilians. Today bombing enemy targets is so much more accurate than in the two World Wars. It just seems terribly sad that so many innocent civilians died as a result of bombing places like London, Coventry, Hamburg, Dresden and so many other places in Europe.

I suppose the one thing I have to thank World War II for is that I met my wonderful wife Margarete and for that I thank God. I was not particularly religious before the war but, like many of my mates, I prayed most nights when I was in Europe and thanked God for my survival. Even now I pray every day and go to church when I can. My health is not good but I thank him for a long and happy life.

Some of my mates were religious and believed in a God of some kind, some didn't and said so. One incident happened which highlighted this.
We were in France on day patrol, I can't remember exactly where, we were under fire from a German sniper and decided to take cover in a church which had been badly damaged. There were six or eight of us with a Sergeant. We all went into the church ruins except one soldier who swore and said he didn't believe in God and that he was going to sit outside and look after himself. After a few minutes we heard the noise of three shells coming at us and exploding followed by screams and shouts from our mate outside. He had been hit and was badly wounded in his arms and a leg and his tin hat had protected him from serious damage to his head. I was a trained first-aider and I took what shrapnel I could out of his leg, bathed the wounds with wine that I always carried and bandaged him up. We took some curtains down from the church windows and some pieces of wood and made a makeshift stretcher. We carried the poor chap as far as we could

but in the end had to help him to hobble along until he was picked up by the medics. I think he did live. Looking back on that incident I don't know if it was just fate that our mate got injured after saying he did not believe in God and the rest of us inside the church were unharmed, but I do know I always had my faith which helped me survive the war. Over 4,000 soldiers from the 15th Scottish were lost but I was one of the lucky few who survived and I will never forget my close mates who died doing their duty.

I remember that not long after this incident an Officer came to see me and said that he had been told by the medics that every time they treated a wounded soldier that I had carried out first aid on their wounds seemed to smell of alcohol and their breath smelt of alcohol. I told him that was because I treated wounds with alcohol. I always carried wine or brandy which I used to nick from shops or bars or wherever I could get it, I never paid for it. I told the Officer that alcohol was a very good antiseptic to treat an open wound with. He asked me where I learnt that and when I told him that it was in the Bible – Jesus had his wounds bathed in alcohol when he was on the cross – the Officer told me to carry on the good work.

I am sometimes asked if I was aware that I shot anyone during the war. We often shot at low-flying German aircraft that attacked us and sometimes we brought them down, but I wasn't directly aware of shooting anyone. Like most soldiers who engaged with the enemy I suppose I did though. However, I do not have any problem with that because, after all, it was a war.

I have also been asked about comrades who were dreadfully wounded, near to death, suffering terribly and asked to be put out of their misery by colleagues. I know this did happen but I never witnessed it. Such an act is possibly a demonstration of the love for one man towards another. It is something I don't really want to think about, it is just another sad part of war.

I am also asked if I was aware or saw any evidence of concentration camps. I do remember that one day at the end of the war we were told about them and one, Wobbelin near Schwerin, was fairly close to where we were. A few of our Officers and Sergeants went to the Camp and some of us were to go the following day. However, because of what they had seen it was decided that we should not go there. They said very little about it, seemed quite shocked and told us not to talk about anything we might have heard. I believe there were mainly Polish, Russian and Jewish prisoners at the camp, thousands had died or been killed and there were about 2,500 survivors in dreadful conditions. Several days later I was asked to make a lot of notice boards, and photographs that had been taken at the Camp were put up on the boards in the town for the local population to see and realise what had been going on. Some of the locals also were made to attend the funerals of prisoners. Some of our Officers attended a church service in Schwerin in remembrance of the prisoners who had tragically died. It was only after the war that I learned the terrible truth about the enormity of what had happened in the Death Camps, but I have never believed that the ordinary German people, even if they had suspected what was happening, could have done anything to stop it.

In this day and age Post Traumatic Stress Disorder is a recognised condition suffered by people who have witnessed dreadful and horrific events, particularly during wartime. During the First and Second World Wars the disorder was not understood as it is now, and although it was accepted that soldiers did suffer mentally from their experiences the condition was generally described as 'Shell Shock' or 'Bomb Happy.' The aftercare for the sufferers was not as it is today – many were put in Mental Institutions and some received electric shock treatment.

The incident involving the dead paratroopers in the trees and other incidents I experienced did affect me a lot, and although I didn't really know at the time, those events did cause me problems after the war.
When Margarete and I came to England to live we settled down to a happy life. I got my old job as a carpenter. At first we lived with my parents and although both accepted her, particularly my Dad, my Mother found it more difficult. Margerete was at home with her all day while I was at work and spoke little English, Mum spoke no German and this caused me some worry. We spent four years living with my parents, but after staying with an Aunt and Uncle for a while, eventually we got our own place.

In 1949 I found I couldn't sleep and my nerves were quite bad. I went to see my Doctor who prescribed medication to help me. That didn't seem to work and so the GP sent me to see a specialist at Worthing Hospital who referred me to a psychiatrist. Over a period of time I had sessions with the psychiatrist and he took me right back to re-live the events that I had found disturbing during the war. Those sessions did help me and I gradually got better. I was advised not to watch war films and even to this day I don't – I admit I do have a laugh at 'Dad's Army' though! I still sometimes have nightmares and I kick out because I think someone is attacking me.

I didn't tell anyone about my treatment as I felt very ashamed, although now I realise there was nothing for me to be ashamed of. I hate November 5th and the sound of exploding fireworks or any loud bangs. I know I am not unusual and there are many ex-soldiers, not only from the World Wars but from other conflicts, who have suffered mentally from war experiences.

I am now eighty six years old, my health is not that good, but as I look back on my life I have a great deal to thank God for .Surviving the war when thousands of young lads didn't, making so many friends, meeting Margarete and being able to enjoy so many years of happy marriage. Yes, I am a very lucky, contented happy man.